OPPOSING
VIEWPOINTS®
SERIES

Garbage and Recycling

Other Books of Related Interest:

Opposing Viewpoints Series
Coal
Pollution

At Issue Series
Green Cities
What Is the Impact of E-Waste?

Global Viewpoints
Air Pollution
Garbage and Recycling

Introducing Issues with Opposing Viewpoints
Energy Alternatives

Issues That Concern You
Climate Change
Consumer Culture
Going Green

"Congress shall make no law . . . abridging the freedom of speech, or of the press."

First Amendment to the US Constitution

The basic foundation of our democracy is the First Amendment guarantee of freedom of expression. The Opposing Viewpoints series is dedicated to the concept of this basic freedom and the idea that it is more important to practice it than to enshrine it.

OPPOSING VIEWPOINTS® SERIES

Garbage and Recycling

Margaret Haerens, Book Editor

GREENHAVEN PRESS
A part of Gale, Cengage Learning

GALE
CENGAGE Learning®

Detroit • New York • San Francisco • New Haven, Conn • Waterville, Maine • London

GALE
CENGAGE Learning·

Elizabeth Des Chenes, *Managing Editor*

© 2012 Greenhaven Press, a part of Gale, Cengage Learning.

Gale and Greenhaven Press are registered trademarks used herein under license.

For more information, contact:
Greenhaven Press
27500 Drake Rd.
Farmington Hills, MI 48331-3535
Or you can visit our Internet site at gale.cengage.com

For product information and technology assistance, contact us at

Gale Customer Support, 1-800-877-4253
For permission to use material from this text or product, submit all requests online at
www.cengage.com/permissions

Further permissions questions can be emailed to permissionrequest@cengage.com

Articles in Greenhaven Press anthologies are often edited for length to meet page requirements. In addition, original titles of these works are changed to clearly present the main thesis and to explicitly indicate the author's opinion. Every effort is made to ensure that Greenhaven Press accurately reflects the original intent of the authors. Every effort has been made to trace the owners of copyrighted material.

Cover image copyright © Sorin Alb/Shutterstock.com

LIBRARY OF CONGRESS CATALOGING-IN-PUBLICATION DATA

Garbage and Recycling / Margaret Haerens, book editor.
   p. cm. -- (Opposing viewpoints)
   Summary: "Garbage and Recycling: Is Garbage a Serious Problem?; Is Recycling Effective?; Is Toxic Waste Disposal a Serious Problem?; What Strategies Will Help Reduce Waste and Save Money?"--Provided by publisher.
   Includes bibliographical references and index.
   ISBN 978-0-7377-5428-5 (hardback) -- ISBN 978-0-7377-5429-2 (paperback)
   1. Refuse and refuse disposal. 2. Recycling (Waste, etc.) 3. Hazardous wastes. I. Haerens, Margaret.
   TD791.G37 2011
   363.72'88--dc23

                                        2011022632

Printed in the United States of America
1 2 3 4 5 6 7 15 14 13 12 11

Contents

Why Consider Opposing Viewpoints?   11

Introduction   14

Chapter 1: Is Garbage a Serious Problem?

Chapter Preface   19

1. The United States Has a Garbage Crisis   21
   Peter Lehner

2. There Is No Garbage Crisis in the United States   25
   Jane Chastain

3. Landfills Are Dangerous   29
   Environment News Service

4. Landfills Are Relatively Safe   33
   Useful-Community-Development.org

5. The Great Pacific Garbage Patch   40
   Is an Environmental Disaster
   Graham Land

6. The Magnitude of the Great Pacific   45
   Garbage Patch Is Overstated
   Jay L. Wile

7. Plastic Bags Are a Huge Waste Problem   50
   and Should Be Banned
   Marc Basnight

8. Plastic Bags Are Useful and Should   55
   Not Be Banned
   Lenore Skenazy

Periodical and Internet Sources Bibliography   59

Chapter 2: Is Recycling Effective?

Chapter Preface   61

1. Recycling Reinforces Social Responsibility 63
   Christal Marx

2. Recycling Encourages Consumption 67
   and Materialism
   GreenMuze.com

3. Recycling Does Not Solve 70
   Environmental Problems
   Anthony B. Bradley

4. Recycling Benefits the Environment 75
   The Economist

5. Mandatory Recycling Wastes Resources 89
   James Thayer

6. Mandatory Recycling Helps Reduce Waste 96
   Chris Bristol

7. Mandatory Recycling Undermines Civil Liberties 101
   Wendy McElroy

8. Pay-As-You-Throw Programs Work 107
   Raphael Gang and Scot Matayoshi

9. Pay-As-You-Throw Programs Do Not Work 112
   Richard Olson Jr.

Periodical and Internet Sources Bibliography 117

Chapter 3: Is Toxic Waste Disposal a Serious Problem?

Chapter Preface 119

1. Nuclear Waste Should Be Reprocessed 121
   William Tucker

2. Nuclear Waste Should Not Be Reprocessed 126
   Union of Concerned Scientists

3. The Yucca Mountain Nuclear Waste Facility   132
   Should Be Closed
   Timothy Noah

4. The Yucca Mountain Nuclear Waste Facility   137
   Should Not Be Closed
   Jack Spencer

5. Fly Ash Landfills Are a Safe Solution   143
   to Coal Ash Waste
   Brock Hill

6. Fly Ash Landfills and Ponds Create   149
   Health Hazards
   Tony Bartelme

7. Recycling E-Waste Is Environmentally Beneficial   158
   Rex Springston

8. Recycling E-Waste Endangers   164
   Third World Countries
   ABC News

Periodical and Internet Sources Bibliography   170

Chapter 4: What Strategies Will Help Reduce Waste and Save Money?

Chapter Preface   172

1. Eliminating Disposable Plastic   174
   Will Decrease Waste
   Daniella Russo

2. Single-Stream Recycling Is Economical and Easy   179
   Kevin Taylor

3. Solar-Powered Trash Compactors Can Make   185
   Trash Collection More Efficient
   Daniel Gross

4. Electrobiochemical Reactors Treat Waste   190
   Efficiently and Cheaply
   Brendon Bosworth

5. Plasma Gasification Successfully Converts   195
   Trash into Energy
   Michael Behar

6. Reprocessing Medical Equipment   208
   Minimizes Waste and Saves Money
   *Gifty Kwakye, Peter Pronovost, and
   Martin A. Makary*

Periodical and Internet Sources Bibliography   219

For Further Discussion   220

Organizations to Contact   222

Bibliography of Books   229

Index   232

Why Consider Opposing Viewpoints?

> "The only way in which a human being can make some approach to knowing the whole of a subject is by hearing what can be said about it by persons of every variety of opinion and studying all modes in which it can be looked at by every character of mind. No wise man ever acquired his wisdom in any mode but this."
>
> *John Stuart Mill*

In our media-intensive culture it is not difficult to find differing opinions. Thousands of newspapers and magazines and dozens of radio and television talk shows resound with differing points of view. The difficulty lies in deciding which opinion to agree with and which "experts" seem the most credible. The more inundated we become with differing opinions and claims, the more essential it is to hone critical reading and thinking skills to evaluate these ideas. Opposing Viewpoints books address this problem directly by presenting stimulating debates that can be used to enhance and teach these skills. The varied opinions contained in each book examine many different aspects of a single issue. While examining these conveniently edited opposing views, readers can develop critical thinking skills such as the ability to compare and contrast authors' credibility, facts, argumentation styles, use of persuasive techniques, and other stylistic tools. In short, the Opposing Viewpoints Series is an ideal way to attain the higher-level thinking and reading skills so essential in a culture of diverse and contradictory opinions.

In addition to providing a tool for critical thinking, Opposing Viewpoints books challenge readers to question their own strongly held opinions and assumptions. Most people form their opinions on the basis of upbringing, peer pressure, and personal, cultural, or professional bias. By reading carefully balanced opposing views, readers must directly confront new ideas as well as the opinions of those with whom they disagree. This is not to simplistically argue that everyone who reads opposing views will—or should—change his or her opinion. Instead, the series enhances readers' understanding of their own views by encouraging confrontation with opposing ideas. Careful examination of others' views can lead to the readers' understanding of the logical inconsistencies in their own opinions, perspective on why they hold an opinion, and the consideration of the possibility that their opinion requires further evaluation.

Evaluating Other Opinions

To ensure that this type of examination occurs, Opposing Viewpoints books present all types of opinions. Prominent spokespeople on different sides of each issue as well as well-known professionals from many disciplines challenge the reader. An additional goal of the series is to provide a forum for other, less known, or even unpopular viewpoints. The opinion of an ordinary person who has had to make the decision to cut off life support from a terminally ill relative, for example, may be just as valuable and provide just as much insight as a medical ethicist's professional opinion. The editors have two additional purposes in including these less known views. One, the editors encourage readers to respect others' opinions—even when not enhanced by professional credibility. It is only by reading or listening to and objectively evaluating others' ideas that one can determine whether they are worthy of consideration. Two, the inclusion of such viewpoints encourages the important critical thinking skill of objectively evaluating an author's credentials and bias. This evaluation will illuminate an author's reasons for taking a particular stance on an issue and will aid in readers' evaluation of the author's ideas.

It is our hope that these books will give readers a deeper understanding of the issues debated and an appreciation of the complexity of even seemingly simple issues when good and honest people disagree. This awareness is particularly important in a democratic society such as ours in which people enter into public debate to determine the common good. Those with whom one disagrees should not be regarded as enemies but rather as people whose views deserve careful examination and may shed light on one's own.

Thomas Jefferson once said that "difference of opinion leads to inquiry, and inquiry to truth." Jefferson, a broadly educated man, argued that "if a nation expects to be ignorant and free . . . it expects what never was and never will be." As individuals and as a nation, it is imperative that we consider the opinions of others and examine them with skill and discernment. The Opposing Viewpoints series is intended to help readers achieve this goal.

David L. Bender and Bruno Leone,
Founders

Introduction

"The proposal to dump nuclear waste at Yucca Mountain threatened the health and safety of Nevadans and people across our nation. Yucca Mountain, which is 90 miles northwest of Las Vegas, is simply not a safe or secure site to store nuclear waste."

—Senator Harry Reid, US senator from Nevada

In the 1970s the United States began to search for a viable site for a nuclear waste repository, a storage location for spent nuclear reactor fuel and other radioactive waste. As commercial nuclear power plants were coming online all over the country to generate much-needed electric power, the problem of how to dispose of spent nuclear reactor fuel was growing. If nuclear power was going to be a key and viable component in America's long-term energy policy, the issue of nuclear waste storage needed to be addressed.

Spent nuclear fuel, which is classified as high-level radioactive waste because it has such high levels of radioactivity, needs to be isolated to protect humans, animal life, and the environment. For such hazardous radioactive material, it is thought to take thousands of years for levels of radioactivity to diminish to the point where it is no longer a threat to human survival. There are a couple of common ways to store it. Most spent nuclear fuel is stored in pools at individual reactor sites. Some spent nuclear fuel is placed in dry cask storage that is kept above ground.

As far back as 1957, the US government decided that a more permanent and stable storage system was needed. That year, the National Academy of Sciences recommended that the best means of protecting the environment and public health and safety would be to dispose of the waste underground, in deep rock. In 1982 the US Congress passed the Nuclear Waste Policy Act, a law that allowed for the building and operating of the repository.

The site chosen for the storage repository was Yucca Mountain, Arizona, located about ninety miles northwest of Las Vegas. The planned repository was designed to store more than seventy thousand metric tons of spent nuclear fuel and high-level radioactive waste underground in deep rock, where it would be held safely for hundreds of thousands of years. In 2006, with the full support of the George W. Bush administration, the project moved forward, with the Department of Energy announcing it would be ready by 2017.

From the beginning, however, there was virulent environmental and political opposition to building a storage repository at Yucca Mountain. Nevadans have consistently opposed it, arguing that the site-selection process was not properly handled and that they should not have to be burdened with a nuclear waste storage facility—particularly when Nevada doesn't even have a nuclear power plant within its borders. Many Nevada officials were worried that the repository would negatively impact the tourist industry. Native Americans maintained the facility would limit access to sacred natural resources. Another key point of contention was safety. The radioactivity of the waste to be stored at Yucca Mountain would not diminish for an estimated ten thousand to one million years into the future, and officials worried that any leak could be extremely dangerous to people and wildlife in the region. Transporting the waste from facilities around the country to Yucca Mountain was also an issue, as spills and accidents could also be extremely hazardous.

Despite mounting political and environmental opposition, the plan to build the storage facility at Yucca Mountain pushed forward in the mid-2000s. However, with the election of

Barack Obama in the 2008 presidential election, momentum in the Yucca Mountain debate began to shift. Obama had campaigned on closing the facility, and after he was elected, he fulfilled that campaign pledge. In July 2009 the US Senate passed a spending bill that effectively cut off funding to the project after twenty-five years and $13.5 billion dollars spent.

Although Obama's decision was applauded by many policy makers, environmental activists, officials, and Nevadans, there was also considerable opposition to the move. After all, billions of dollars had been spent; resources had been invested; and studies supported the decision that Yucca Mountain was the best option for a nuclear waste storage repository. Moreover, the problem still remained: The United States urgently needed a long-term solution for storing high-level radioactive waste from nuclear power plants.

In 2011 Republican lawmakers seem poised to reopen the debate on the Yucca Mountain facility. As part of a broad plan to expand the use of nuclear energy in the United States, they included a provision to force the Nuclear Regulatory Commission to complete a review of the Yucca Mountain site "without political interference."

The debate over Yucca Mountain embodies the problems with coming up with a viable and popular waste policy. Whether it is landfills or nuclear waste storage facilities, individuals and policy makers have a "not-in-my-backyard" attitude. It is perfectly understandable that people don't want noisy, ugly, smelly, and potentially hazardous waste disposal sites in their neighborhood; but such facilities have to go somewhere. Many individuals would economically benefit from a facility at Yucca Mountain because it allows for the storage of spent nuclear fuel, thereby facilitating the greater use of nuclear energy. However, there are also health and environmental consequences associated with the use of nuclear fuel—or plastics, coal, tires, diapers, and other waste. Government officials have to consider all of these factors when making such important decisions.

The debate over Yucca Mountain illuminates broader issues of waste removal and storage policy that are examined in *Opposing Viewpoints: Garbage and Recycling*. The viewpoints in this book explore the consequences of waste policy and consider potential waste and recycling strategies in the following chapters: "Is Garbage a Serious Problem?" "Is Recycling Effective?" "Is Toxic Waste Disposal a Serious Problem?" and "What Strategies Will Help Reduce Waste and Save Money?" The information presented in this volume will provide insight into some of the recent controversies surrounding landfills, nuclear waste reprocessing, e-cycling, mandatory recycling, and medical waste reprocessing.

CHAPTER 1

Is Garbage a Serious Problem?

Chapter Preface

In 2005 San Francisco officials began looking for a viable strategy for reducing the estimated 180 million plastic bags distributed to shoppers in the city every year. Although a convenient way to carry groceries and other items, plastic bags were ending up in landfills as well as in trees, waterways, and in drainage systems. Plus, there were considerable environmental concerns. Most plastic bags are made from petroleum, a nonrenewable resource that is expensive, hazardous to supply, and reinforces US dependence on foreign oil. Experts estimate it takes 430,000 gallons of oil to manufacture 100 million bags. In landfills, plastic bags can take up to one thousand years to decompose and deposit toxic chemicals into the soil. In the water, environmentalists contend that plastic bags strangle marine life; if ingested, they could choke an animal to death or cause starvation. Certainly, San Francisco officials thought, there had to be a way to encourage the use of recyclable or compostable sacks instead of plastic bags.

One solution they considered was a seventeen-cent tax on each bag, making cloth bags and recyclable sacks a better deal economically. The tax, however, encountered heavy opposition from the California Grocers Association who did not want to shoulder the costs of transitioning to a new system. A compromise was reached: Large supermarkets would reduce the number of bags they gave shoppers in 2006 by 10 million. When the Grocers Association reported a drop of only 7.6 million that next year, San Francisco officials decided to take stronger measures to cut the number of plastic bags in their city.

In March 2007 San Francisco became the first American city to outlaw the use of plastic checkout bags in large supermarkets and pharmacies. Instead, stores had to provide compostable bags made of corn starch or recyclable paper bags.

San Francisco was not the first city in the world to enact legislation to curb plastic bag use. In 2002 Ireland passed a tax on plastic bags: Customers were charged a fee for every plastic bag they used at the checkout counter. Almost immediately, there was a 94 percent drop in plastic bag use. The tax also raised revenues of millions of euros that were used for environmental projects around the country. The tax was so successful, in fact, it was doubled in 2009 in hopes of almost completely eliminating plastic bag use altogether.

Bangladesh completely outlawed the use of plastic bags in 2002 after evidence showed that they were responsible for clogging the nation's drainage systems and causing the terrible floods of 1998 that submerged two-thirds of the country. Other countries also took action with plastic bag taxes or bans, including Greece, Taiwan, China, India, Australia, Italy, South Africa, and Israel. Worldwatch Institute reports that China's decision to ban plastic bags in 2008 cut demand by approximately 40 billion bags, reduced plastic bag usage there by 66 percent, and saved 1.6 million tons of petroleum.

San Francisco's success soon caught the eye of other American cities and municipalities dealing with the effects of plastic bag pollution. A number of other major cities implemented taxes or bans, including San Jose, California; Washington, DC; and Westport, Connecticut. In addition, small towns and counties have also found ways to limit plastic bag use.

Policy concerning plastic bag pollution is one of the issues discussed in the following chapter, which examines the garbage crisis in the United States. Other topics under examination are the danger of landfills and the severity of the Great Pacific Garbage Patch.

| *"We're drowning in a sea of our own
waste."*

The United States Has a Garbage Crisis

Peter Lehner

Peter Lehner is the executive director of the Natural Resources Defense Council (NRDC). In the following viewpoint, he observes that the explosion of global production and consumption has resulted in a global garbage crisis. Lehner argues that Americans have to begin addressing this problem in a logical and comprehensive way—starting with examining our own personal consumption habits.

As you read, consider the following questions:

1. What is Thomas Malthus known for saying, according to Lehner?

2. How many plastic beverage bottles does the viewpoint state are used in the United States every five minutes?

3. How many aluminum cans are used in the United States every thirty seconds, according to the author?

Peter Lehner, "We're Drowning in Our Own Trash," *Switchboard: Natural Resources Defense Council Staff Blog*, July 11, 2008. Reproduced with permission from the Natural Resources Defense Council.

Thomas Malthus [a nineteenth-century English scholar] has suddenly become popular again. While Americans are concerned about fuel prices, much of the rest of the world is concerned about food prices. In countries like Egypt and Bangladesh, and in regions of Africa, riots have erupted over a shortage of food. In other countries, like China and India, when rice is shipped, it's shipped under the protection of armed guards.

Global production simply can't keep up with global consumption. And so people are asking: Was Malthus right?

Malthus, an economist and demographer from the 19th century, is known for predicting that population growth moves more quickly than the expansion of food production. As the former moves geometrically, and the latter arithmetically, it's inevitable that population overcomes production. As a result, Malthus predicted, people will starve.

Many experts now believe that the 19th century proved Malthus incorrect. The Green Revolution increased global food production, helping it keep pace with global population growth. It allowed us to keep consuming.

But with anything you produce, you also have waste. And, given the growing consumption, unless one is very careful about production technologies, you have waste on a massive scale. As photographs by Chris Jordan and our daily experience of taking out the trash and seeing litter everywhere can testify, our consumption of goods leads to an overwhelming volume of trash. So much so that the scale of the numbers can be difficult to comprehend. Consider some numbers Jordan uses:

- Two million plastic beverage bottles are used in the US every five minutes.

- 1.14 million brown paper supermarket bags are used in the US every hour.

"From the Stone Age to the GarbAge," cartoon by Jason Love. www.CartoonStock.com.
Copyright © Jason Love. Reproduction rights obtainable from www.CartoonStock.com.

- 426,000 cell phones are retired in the US every day.

- While 106,000 aluminum cans are used in the US every thirty seconds.

And that's just the waste we can see. Waste gases from power plants are filling the air that we breathe, leading to the early deaths of tens of thousands of Americans and hundreds of thousands or millions around the world. Invisible carbon dioxide is turning the oceans so acidic that shellfish are having a harder time growing their shells while it changes our entire planet's climate.

The point here is pretty clear. We're drowning in a sea of our own waste.

This point changes the way we have to understand Malthus. For him, it was a two-way balance between consumption and production. Now, it's a three-way balance between production, consumption, and waste.

And it's no longer simply a question of whether we can have another Green Revolution to increase production, because even if we did that, we would only increase our waste problem.

We have to begin addressing this question of waste. If we are to feed more people—and we will have to, given predictions of global population growths—than we should also free more people of the sea of garbage and poison and waste our production has created.

Part of this will be to examine our own, personal consumption habits. Each of us should find ways to reduce our waste, whether it's by bringing lunch to work, or by using cloth bags at the grocery store, or by driving smaller cars. Whatever it is that works for you, I'd urge you to try it.

Will that be enough? Certainly not. But it is a start. A start to be expanded on every day.

> *"There is no garbage crisis: never has been; never will be—especially if the free market is allowed to handle the process."*

There Is No Garbage Crisis in the United States

Jane Chastain

Jane Chastain is an author and political commentator. In the following viewpoint, she maintains that it is a myth that there is a garbage crisis. In fact, she argues, the problem with garbage is that the government has passed regulations that interfere with what people are allowed to throw away and recycle. Chastain notes that if government got out of the garbage business and let the free market dictate recycling and trash processes in the United States, more people would be motivated to recycle and economic wealth would increase.

As you read, consider the following questions:

1. According to a study by Daniel K. Benjamin, the garbage trade raises US wealth by how much?

Jane Chastain, "Let's Talk Trash," WorldNetDaily.com, February 11, 2010. Reproduced by permission.

2. How many toxic substances did the Environmental Protection Agency find in the paper recycling process, according to the viewpoint?

3. In what sector does the author say all the profitable recycling opportunities are?

L et's get down and dirty. Now don't get excited. This [viewpoint] is not the least bit off-color or X-rated. I'm talking about your garbage.

Do you recycle? Do you meticulously separate your cans, bottles and plastic containers from the paper and cardboard?

The world is going green, but when it comes to our garbage, what we have been conditioned to do or feel compelled to do or—worse still—are coerced to do may end up hurting, not helping, the environment.

There is nothing inherently wrong with recycling. It's been going on since the beginning of time and is as old as, well, garbage itself.

In urban areas, there must be an orderly and sanitary way to dispose of trash. Only in the last 25 years, however, have state and federal regulators gotten involved in the methods used in trash disposal.

The Garbage Crisis Myth

Presently, the nation is preoccupied with recycling. Much of it is counterproductive and based on misinformation. Thanks to Daniel K. Benjamin, a professor of economics at Clemson University, and PERC, the Property and Environment Research Center, for a recent study that examined the "Eight Great Myths of Recycling." They are as follows:

1. Our garbage will bury us.

2. Our garbage will poison us.

3. Packaging is the problem.

4. We must achieve trash independence.

5. We squander irreplaceable resources when we don't recycle.

6. Recycling always protects the environment.

7. Recycling saves resources.

8. Without forced recycling mandates, there wouldn't be recycling.

There is no garbage crisis: never has been; never will be—especially if the free market is allowed to handle the process. Government has a role to play in regulating where our landfills can be located and making sure that they are safe for the environment. However, when it comes to dictating what we can dispose of and what we must recycle, this is going way too far.

There is great truth to the saying, "One person's trash is another person's treasure." Throughout the world, it is the poor who benefit most from the scavenging process. Likewise, here in the U.S., it is the less affluent, less densely populated areas that benefit most from the business of garbage disposal. According to the Benjamin study, this trade in trash is driven by widely varying disposal costs and inexpensive transportation. The garbage trade raises our wealth as a nation by at least $4 billion. There is no shortage of landfills, and the modern landfill is not dangerous. In fact, it is often more expensive and more costly to the environment to recycle than to send those products to a landfill.

The Problems with Recycling

Recycling is a manufacturing process, and it has an environmental impact. The U.S. Office of Technology Assessment says it is "usually not clear whether secondary manufacturing produces less pollution per ton of material processed than primary manufacturing processes."

Let's look at paper. The Environmental Protection Agency [EPA] found that there were only five toxic substances found in the virgin paper process, while there are eight in the recycling process. The EPA found there are 12 toxic substances common with both processes but, among the 12, all but one was more prevalent in the recycling process.

To be sure, recycling-based secondary manufacturing generally uses less energy and consumes less raw materials. However, all raw material and energy savings evaporated when PERC compared the true costs of recycling versus other forms of disposal.

In communities where curbside recycling is mandated, it requires more trucks to collect the same amount of waste. This requires more iron and coal mining, more steel and rubber manufacturing and more petroleum, which produces more air pollution. All the associated costs are passed along to consumers and taxpayers. Yes, many states and local communities subsidize their recycling programs and hide the true costs in an attempt to prove these programs are cost effective.

It is not surprising to discover that all the profitable opportunities for recycling have been provided by the private sector. This type of recycling dwarfs all government recycling programs. Informed, voluntary recycling conserves resources and raises our wealth. However, things like bottle and can deposit laws—which artificially raise the value of these items to 5 or 10 cents, when in actuality they are worth only a penny or less—induces many to engage in a wasteful activity which consumes valuable time and resources that could be put to better use.

Bottom line: Market prices will, in fact, cause companies and individuals to recycle their own and other people's trash. This, in turn, provides the greater benefit to the environment and all concerned.

> "TCE, an industrial chemical disposed at the Dickson [County] Landfill . . . poses an imminent and substantial endangerment to human health and the environment."

Landfills Are Dangerous

Environment News Service

The Environment News Service (ENS) provides news coverage of original stories related to the environment as well as a press release distribution service called World-Wire. In the following viewpoint, Environment News Service (ENS) reports on a lawsuit filed against the county and city governments in Dickson, Tennessee, after a landfill there was linked to human and environmental health hazards. The Natural Resources Defense Council and two residents of of Dickson, plaintiffs in the lawsuit, allege that studies have shown that there are certain health risks associated with the chemicals being leaked from the landfill, including increased rates of cancer, and there is a significant cost to the environment as well.

"Water Contamination Suit Filed Against Dickson County, Tennessee," Environment News Service, March 10, 2008. Reproduced by permission.

As you read, consider the following questions:

1. According to the viewpoint, who is filing the water contamination lawsuit against the Dickson County and city governments?

2. What is trichloroethylene (TCE), according to the author?

3. What are some of the health and environmental effects of the polluted drinking water in Dickson County, according to the viewpoint?

The Natural Resources Defense Council and two residents of Dickson, Tennessee, have filed a lawsuit against the Dickson County and city governments. They allege that trichloroethylene, TCE, an industrial chemical disposed at the Dickson [County] Landfill that has been linked to neurological and developmental harm and cancer, poses an imminent and substantial endangerment to human health and the environment.

Dickson County Landfill

Dickson, a town of some 12,000 people, is located about 35 miles west of Nashville.

The Dickson County Landfill, 74 acres off Eno Road, sits within 500 to 2,000 feet of approximately 40 homes, most owned by blacks.

One African American family in particular, the Holts, a family of black landowners, has been especially harmed by the chemical. Many Holt family members are struggling with cancer and other illnesses, and two of its members are plaintiffs in this lawsuit.

The environmental group and Sheila Holt-Orsted and Beatrice Holt allege that TCE pollution has seeped beneath the landfill to underlying groundwater and has spread through a large area of Dickson County.

The Dangers of Landfills

In 2008, a survey of landfills found that 82 percent of surveyed landfill cells had leaks, while 41 percent had a leak larger than 1 square foot.

Newer, lined landfills leak in narrow plumes, making leaks only detectable if they reach landfill monitoring wells. Both old and new landfills are usually located near large bodies of water, making detection of leaks and their cleanup difficult.

Incinerators are a major source of 210 different dioxin compounds, plus mercury, cadmium, nitrous oxide, hydrogen chloride, sulfuric acid, fluorides, and particulate matter small enough to lodge permanently in the lungs.

In 2007, the EPA [US Environmental Protection Agency] acknowledged that despite recent tightening of emission standards for waste incineration power plants, the waste-to-energy process still "creates significant emissions, including trace amounts of hazardous air pollutants."

"Waste and Recycling Facts," Clean Air Council, 2010.

Landfills Leak Toxins

TCE contamination has rendered water from wells and springs as far as two to three miles from the landfill unfit for human consumption, the plaintiffs claim.

Polluted spring water is flowing directly into the West Piney River, a fishing stream and a major source of drinking water for the Water Authority of Dickson County. Several square miles of Dickson County have been recognized as an "imminent threat" area by the county.

TCE contamination above drinking water limits, and orders of magnitude above U.S. Environmental Protection Agency screening levels for drinking water, has been found in at least one well even beyond that threat area.

Contamination May Be Increasing

In some areas, this TCE contamination may be growing worse, the plaintiffs claim, but the city and county have not done anything to remove the contamination.

"Some two decades after TCE was first detected in nearby drinking water sources, those responsible have not even fully characterized the present extent and likely future spread of the contamination. Defendants have, in effect, surrendered the ground and surface water of Dickson County to the slow spread of an invisible and toxic chemical," the complainants said in a statement.

The complaint asks the court to require the defendants to investigate the present extent and future spread of TCE contamination from the landfill in the soil, surface water, and groundwater of Dickson County; to remediate and abate TCE contamination.

Holt-Orsted has undergone six surgeries and chemotherapy for breast cancer. The Holts originally filed lawsuits in 2003 and 2004, naming the city and county of Dickson and the state of Tennessee, and claiming the family was a victim of negligence that resulted in their cancers and other health problems.

Attorneys for the county and state deny the claims in the earlier lawsuits.

> "Many parts of the world would have a
> much safer and cleaner environment if
> only they had a landfill."

Landfills Are Relatively Safe

Useful-Community-Development.org

Useful-Community-Development.org is a website that posts articles about and analyses of urban planning and development topics. In the following viewpoint, the writer describes the key role of landfills in US waste policy and traces the US government's efforts to regulate landfills to limit pollution to groundwater and neighborhoods. The writer also chronicles the search for alternatives to sanitary landfills and the movement to reclaim defunct landfills to make them into golf courses or parks. The author recommends to neighborhoods that individuals petition local governments to transform nonfunctioning landfills into simple locales with plenty of grass and native plants for recreation purposes.

As you read, consider the following questions:

1. What does the author indicate is the useful life of a landfill?

"Sanitary Landfills Entomb Your Solid Waste Forever," Useful-Community-Development.org, 2010. Reproduced by permission.

2. Which does the viewpoint state that most landfills are: dry or wet?

3. What alternative strategy is central to the aim of building less landfills, according to the author?

Sanitary landfills are places where solid waste is disposed of, permanently or temporarily. The sanitary modifier indicates that there is an engineered attempt to contain the waste and its impacts to the facility itself, and not to spill over onto adjacent land, the air, or groundwater. This has been the most common method of waste disposal in recent decades in the U.S. and in many other parts of the world as well.

The term landfill may be applied, perhaps inappropriately, also to a transfer station, where garbage trucks temporarily deliver solid waste until it is transferred to the larger facility by truck. A landfill also may be a private facility used by only one or a small group of industries.

The Benefits of a Landfill

Before we start criticizing landfills, we should keep in mind that they were a progressive reform in their day. For instance, in the mid twentieth century the U.S. started regulating landfills to make them safer for neighbors and to groundwater and air.

Many parts of the world would have a much safer and cleaner environment if only they had a landfill. In many places on earth, dump cleanup should be the first goal. Visitors, please tell us some success stories about such projects.

At any rate, when the U.S. began regulating practices, new requirements included liners often consisting of compacted clays, thick plastic, and possibly solid rock, supposedly protecting the groundwater underneath; requirements for daily covering of all solid waste with clean dirt or alternatives such as foam; measures designed to prevent storm water runoff from unburied waste; and a pipe collection system designed to capture leachate (liquids leaching—leaking slowly—out of the decomposing solid waste) for treatment before it reaches soil or water.

Solid waste is spread in layers and compacted soon after it is deposited on the sanitary landfill site, to keep the area of what is known as the daily cell as small as possible. This covering of the cell reduces the amount of vermin attracted to the site. Cells are devised either through digging a trench and filling it, constructing a ramp along which solid waste will be dumped, or setting aside a disposal area within the landfill.

Monitoring wells are dug outside the site so that any groundwater contamination will be identified as it happens.

Landfills often have a useful life of 15 to 20 years, although this varies widely depending on the characteristics of the site, the degree to which waste is compacted, the disposal and recycling habits of the local population, and regulatory requirements. State environmental agencies set the requirements for sanitary landfills in the U.S., although the EPA (U.S. Environmental Protection Agency) sets a minimum standard below which states cannot go.

These facilities also are categorized as either dry landfills, in which the goal is to segregate the waste as much as possible from air; or wet landfills, in which air is allowed and the leachate even recirculated to encourage more decomposition. Most of us have heard various scandals about what was sitting in the landfill and didn't decompose, so it's important to realize that most landfills are dry landfills and not really designed to decompose its contents. The wet landfill is an experimental attempt to make sure that more of the solid waste actually ends up returning to soil.

Locating Sanitary Landfills

Sometimes landfills take advantage of existing pits, such as those resulting from an extraction activity, or valleys. Often, however, the solid waste is simply stacked on the ground, building up a large mound over time. They should be located away from rivers and creeks and in areas where earthquakes are unlikely. Obviously wetlands and habitat supporting endangered species should be avoided, as well as ordinary floodplains. Since birds are attracted to landfills almost regardless of how well operated they are, sanitary landfills are not placed too close to airports.

The transportation network to deliver the solid waste to the site by truck or rail must be robust, and neighbors who might object ideally should be scarce. State and local regulatory authorities also may impact the siting of sanitary landfills.

Understandably, residential neighbors usually are highly opposed, even if only because of increased smelly truck traffic. Noise from compaction and the possibility of rodents and other pests are also problems, along with general fears that the facility will not be operated properly and that health and environmental concerns will surface when it is too late to do anything about them. Therefore the search for alternatives has accelerated.

Alternatives to Sanitary Landfills

Alternatives center around a waste reduction strategy, which at best postpones the time when new sanitary landfills must be constructed in a region.

Incineration (burning in a specially designed apparatus) in some form has been a viable alternative for decades, but no one form of incinerator has emerged as the clear leader.

While the visionary claim that we should strive for zero waste is a worthwhile goal, it is unlikely that in the near future waste will be eliminated entirely, through reuse, repurposing, recycling, and natural decomposition. So some consideration of sanitary landfills is likely to be a factor of urban life and rural regions for some time to come.

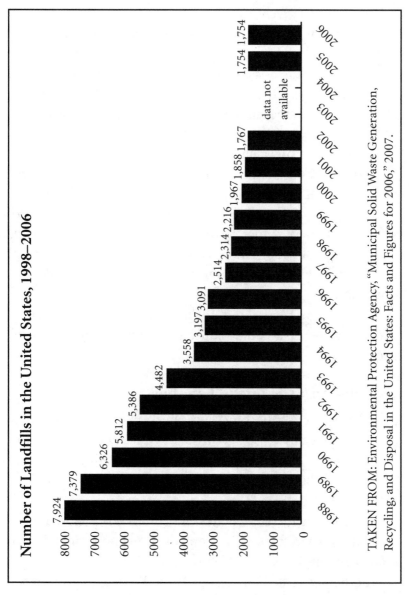

Number of Landfills in the United States, 1998–2006

1988 7,924
1989 7,379
1990 6,326
1991 5,812
1992 5,386
1993 4,482
1994 3,558
1995 3,197
1996 3,091
1997 2,514
1998 2,314
1999 2,216
2000 1,967
2001 1,858
2002 1,767
2003 data not available
2004 data not available
2005 1,754
2006 1,754

TAKEN FROM: Environmental Protection Agency, "Municipal Solid Waste Generation, Recycling, and Disposal in the United States: Facts and Figures for 2006," 2007.

However, recycling, including mandatory home pickup recycling, can make a major dent in the amount of material deposited in the landfill. More effort needs to be expended to make disposal of batteries, computers, televisions, and other electronic components more convenient. Some locations make hazardous waste disposal, including paint, chemicals, gasoline, and the like, relatively easy, and others have only occasional pickups or times and places where citizens can deliver their own hazardous waste.

Hazardous waste is a bad actor in sanitary landfills, and we can only urge our local authorities to be more industrious in assuring that recyclables and hazardous materials don't wind up in sanitary landfills. Electronic waste recycling needs to become more prevalent as well.

And then householders could do much more to compost their waste; almost any organic matter, from yard waste to food scraps to egg shells and fish bones, eventually will decompose into a very nice fertilizer. Find yourself an attractive plastic composter that allows easy and nonmanual turning of the material while it disintegrates. (And remember to add coffee grounds.)

And see our page about construction materials recycling, an exciting area that could reduce the landfill burden substantially.

Reclamation of Sanitary Landfills

Landfills frequently become golf courses or parks after they have been officially closed according to a fairly elaborate set of EPA standards. These include sealing the top with a very dense clay cap and digging a trench around the base to capture any rainwater.

There is considerable interest in "mining" our closed landfills, but thus far there is no conclusive method for doing so in an economically efficient manner.

Another green use of former landfill sites being discussed is for solar arrays (groups of solar collectors mounted on poles). The arguments for such a consideration are that typically transportation and zoning are appropriate. One of the first considerations for investigating such a reuse would be the proximity of the site to a three-phase portion of the electrical grid.

It's rather common to see landfills end up as parks. Recently land development has occurred on top of former sanitary landfills, including a California office park. However, when buildings are constructed atop a former landfill, methane gas extraction methods must be utilized to assure there is no explosion hazard. So it's unlikely that this trend will gain much in popularity, with the exception of areas where land values and demand for commercial spaces are extremely high.

Sometimes even during operation, one of the two gases commonly generated by sanitary landfills, methane, can be tapped as a source of energy. Vertical pipes are sunk into the landfill pit to capture the methane. If it is not converted to electricity, generally it is simply burned off. The second common gas, by the way, is carbon dioxide.

Post-closure monitoring of sanitary landfills is absolutely essential and regulated by law in the U.S.

My advice to neighborhoods is to urge your local authorities to stay conventional, plant it in grass or native plantings and make a park, agricultural land, or wildlife preserve. But maybe skip the water feature.

> *"What is most ecologically dangerous about the [Great Pacific] Garbage Patch may not be the enormous eyesore of swirling milk jugs and the pitiful sight of sea turtles choking on discarded magic markers, but rather what can't be seen."*

The Great Pacific Garbage Patch Is an Environmental Disaster

Graham Land

Graham Land is a contributor to GreenFudge.org. In the following viewpoint, he explains the formation of the Great Pacific Garbage Patch and investigates just how serious of a problem it is. Land asserts that the real problem is that degraded plastic is being consumed by marine life and is having a serious effect on the health of the food chain, including humans. Land concludes that the only way to solve the problem is to prevent future waste from being generated and disposed of by using less plastic and recycling more.

Graham Land, "The Great Pacific Garbage Patch: The Parabolic Toilet of the Environment," GreenFudge.org, October 11, 2010. Reproduced by permission.

As you read, consider the following questions:

1. What is the North Pacific Subtropical Gyre, as described in the viewpoint?

2. According to studies, how much has the amount of plastic in marine environments increased every two to three years over the past decade?

3. According to Captain Charles J. Moore, the amount of plastic in the central Pacific outweighs zooplankton by what ratio?

In the middle of the Pacific Ocean there is a maelstrom of debris twice the size of Texas. It has been affectionately given a variety of clever names: the Great Pacific Garbage Patch, the Sea of Trash, the Eastern Garbage Patch, the Asian Trash Trail and (my personal favorite) the Trash Vortex. It is, in short a spiraling swirl of rushing refuse, mostly of the non-biodegradable plastic variety: shampoo bottles, grocery bags, disposable razors, toys . . . you know, stuff made out of plastic, which unfortunately, means just about everything these days. The Plastic Swirl is so big, it even has its own website (cough).

The Great Pacific Garbage Patch is formed by currents from the North Pacific Subtropical Gyre, a mammoth whirlpool of ocean currents and wind, which lies between the Pacific coasts of North America and Asia. This vortex is caused in part by what's known as the Coriolis effect—famous for its presumed (and erroneous) influence on the direction the water in your toilet spins when you flush it, depending on which hemisphere you happen to be in—and vorticity, which is, in layman's terms, the tendency for water to swirl. The Patch lies at the epicenter of the Gyre, which itself takes up most of the Pacific Ocean, covering a surface area of 34 million square kilometers or 10 million square miles.

According to a documentary film called *Plastic Debris, Rivers to Sea* by the Algalita Marine Research Foundation, a non-

Proposed Methods to Clean Up the Garbage Patch

The leading contender is a process called pyrolysis, a form of turning waste into oil or other forms of energy without combustion. By heating input—in this case, floating globs of plastic—upwards of 550 degrees Fahrenheit in a vacuum, much of the waste breaks down. Further processing then converts the substance to a form of synthetic oil.

Daniel Stone, "The Great Pacific Cleanup,"
Newsweek, December 10, 2009.

profit research and educational organization based in Long Beach, California, studies in the coastal waters of Japan have shown that the amount of plastic in marine environments has increased 10 times every two to three years over the past decade. What's more, the overall composition of marine debris in all the oceans of the world is about 60–80% plastic. So this is not just an American, Asian or Pacific environmental problem. It's worldwide.

There are in fact five major ocean-wide gyres: in the North Atlantic, South Atlantic, North Pacific, South Pacific, and Indian Ocean. According to Greenpeace, the Sargasso Sea, a large part of the Atlantic lying between Europe and the Americas, "is a well-known slow circulation area in the Atlantic, and research there has also demonstrated high concentrations of plastic particles present in the water."

How Serious Is the Problem?

Starting to feel depressed? Well, since the Garbage Patch is located pretty far from any significant landmass, at least you won't normally have to look at it. However, if you should happen to be sailing your private yacht from the California coast to Hawaii, it's unavoidable. You're expecting a relaxing voyage through an unspoiled tropical ocean paradise, but suddenly find yourself surrounded by an endless flotilla of waste consisting of billions of plastic bags, bottles and the heads of Cabbage Patch Kids. Remember those?

Captain Charles [J.] Moore, founder of Algalita, found just such an ecological nightmare on his way back from a boat race in 1997. He was so struck by the enormity of the environmental catastrophe he was inspired to let the world know about it. Captain Moore has since published two major scientific research papers concerning marine pollution. One shocking result of his research was that the amount of plastic in the central Pacific outweighs zooplankton by 6 to 1. Zooplankton is a broad term used to collectively refer to all the tiny animals that live in the oceans, seas and other bodies of water. They include microscopic animals, shrimp-like krill and other crustaceans, certain mollusks and baby fish. Zooplankton plays a crucial role in the ecology of our oceans, and it is under threat from plastics.

You see, what is most ecologically dangerous about the Garbage Patch may not be the enormous eyesore of swirling milk jugs and the pitiful sight of sea turtles choking on discarded magic markers, but rather what can't be seen. The biggest problem with plastic is not that it just sticks around in its original molded form, such as a creepy doll's head or a pair of Hawaiian flip flops, but that it degrades into invisible tiny floating beads the size and shape of small plankton. And it's in this way that the plastic really enters the ecosystem, by literally entering the bodies of sea life. Certain marine animals—particularly jellyfish—eat plankton, and many marine birds and sea turtles in turn eat jellyfish. This results in serious nutritional deficiencies, hormonal problems and toxicity for these animals and any others—including humans—connected to them via the food chain. Oh yeah, the little plastic beads are also full of pollutants absorbed from the seawater. Now do you see why Oprah was so shocked?

Are There Viable Solutions?

So is there any solution to the environmental fiasco known as the Great Pacific Garbage Patch? The Environmental Cleanup Coalition has what seems to be a good, albeit ambitious plan, although in an article for the July 2008 issue of *Discover* magazine, Captain Moore himself is decidedly more pessimistic about actually cleaning up the swirl. The only "solution" according to him would be to prevent additional debris from getting into the ocean. This would ultimately mean using a lot less plastic, disposing of it more responsibly and recycling as much as possible.

So the next time you're swimming in the Caribbean or lounging on a beach in Corfu [Greece], please don't chuck your empty Evian bottles into the sea. And if your beach ball accidently rolls into the ocean and starts to float away, go and get it, or it may end up killing some cute dolphin or a blue whale, not to mention swirling around in a nightmarish Trash Vortex in the middle of our most vital of resources.

> "I am not saying that the plastic in the Great Pacific Garbage Patch is no big deal. It most certainly is. In fact, that's what makes this fraud so insidious."

The Magnitude of the Great Pacific Garbage Patch Is Overstated

Jay L. Wile

Jay L. Wile is a textbook author and blogger. In the following viewpoint, he asserts that the size of the Great Pacific Garbage Patch has been so exaggerated that it will be eventually dismissed as just another environmental extremist scare. Wile argues that such exaggeration has hindered attempts to deal with what is a serious problem because it gives outsiders a reason to downplay and even dismiss it. He provides evidence of research conducted on the garbage patch that illustrates the true scope and precise nature of the problem; he claims this is what has been sorely lacking in media coverage of the issue to date.

As you read, consider the following questions:

1. According to Wile, how large did Curtis Ebbesmeyer estimate the size of the garbage patch to be?

Jay L. Wile, "Exaggeration About the Great Pacific Garbage Patch," blog.drwile.com, January 11, 2011. Reproduced by permission of the author.

2. How large did Angelicque White estimate the size of the garbage patch to be, according to the viewpoint?

3. As stated by Wile, how does White believe the plastic can be beneficial to microorganisms in the ocean?

[On my blog] I promised to discuss two scientific frauds that have recently come to light. The first had to do with research related to vaccines. The second one is the topic of this [viewpoint], and it has to do with an environmental issue. The environmental issue is a real one, but unfortunately, it has been exaggerated to such an extent that many will pass it off as just another environmental extremist scare now that the *science* related to it is better understood. To get an idea of the exaggeration, you can click on the YouTube video and see how *Good Morning America* reported on it.

The Great Pacific Garbage Patch

The man being interviewed in the video is oceanographer Charles J. Moore. He is generally credited for discovering the "Great Pacific Garbage Patch," which is a real environmental problem. Oceans have constant circular currents called gyres. When a bit of plastic gets caught in such a current, the current tends to trap it there. Over time, this leads to a large concentration of plastic in that area of the ocean.

In general, most ocean travelers avoid the gyres, as they are a nuisance to navigate through and do not hold a wealth of the kind of ocean life people typically want to see or harvest. However, he and his team decided to travel through the gyre that exists in the North Pacific. He calls it a "subtropical high," and here is his description as found in the journal *Natural History*.

> Yet as I gazed from the deck at the surface of what ought to have been a pristine ocean, I was confronted, as far as the eye could see, with the sight of plastic. It seemed unbelievable, but I never found a clear spot. In the week it took to

How Big Are the "Garbage Patches"?

The reported size and mass of these "patches" have differed from media article to article. Due to the limited sample size, as well as a tendency for observing ships to explore only areas thought to concentrate debris, there is really no accurate estimate on the size or mass of the "garbage patch" or any other concentrations of marine debris in the open ocean. Additionally, many oceanographic features do not have distinct boundaries or a permanent extent, and thus the amount of marine debris (both number and weight) in this zone would be very difficult to measure accurately.

NOAA Marine Debris Program,
"De-Mystifying the 'Great Pacific Garbage Patch,'" 2010.

cross the subtropical high, no matter what time of day I looked, plastic debris was floating everywhere: bottles, bottle caps, wrappers, fragments.

This is what was eventually named "The Great Pacific Garbage Patch." In his article, Moore says that another marine researcher, Curtis Ebbesmeyer, estimates the size of the garbage patch to be roughly that of the state of Texas. He and some colleagues also published a paper that supposedly measured the mass of plastic found in the Great Pacific Garbage Patch and found that it is *six times the mass of the plankton found there.*

Now all this seems incredibly dire. However, it is nothing more than a fraud.

Investigating the Patch

Angelicque White is a serious marine scientist at Oregon State University. She has been studying what the data actually say about the Great Pacific Garbage Patch, and she finds that neither Moore's description nor Ebbesmeyer's estimate is consistent with the data. First, she says:

> The amount of plastic out there isn't trivial. . . . But using the highest concentrations ever reported by scientists produces a patch that is a small fraction of the state of Texas.

In fact, she finds that the fraction is about 0.01. Yes, rather than being as big as the state of Texas, it is about 1% the size of that great state.

How does she know this? Because she has looked at what serious scientists have reported in the literature, and she has actually participated in one of the few expeditions that has tried to accurately measure the amount of debris in the patch. Her interest is to determine the plastic's effect on the microorganisms that live in the ocean.

Speaking of microorganisms, what about Moore's figure of plastic outweighing plankton by a factor of six to one?

> We have data that allow us to make reasonable estimates; we don't need the hyperbole. Given the observed concentration of plastic in the North Pacific, it is simply inaccurate to state that plastic outweighs plankton. . . .

And what is the plastic's effect on the microorganisms in the ocean? It's not very clear. For example, plastic is known to absorb toxic chemicals. In her research she has found that plastic is actually "prime real estate" for *some* microorganisms, because it absorbs toxins that would otherwise harm them. Of course, that doesn't mean it is good for the ecosystem as a whole. As she says:

> On one hand, these plastics may help remove toxins from the water. . . . On the other hand, these same toxin-laden particles may be ingested by fish and seabirds. Plastic clearly does not belong in the ocean.

In the end, here's what she says regarding the best way to visualize the Great Pacific Garbage Patch:

If we were to filter the surface area of the ocean equivalent to a football field in waters having the highest concentration (of plastic) ever recorded ... the amount of plastic recovered would not even extend to the 1-inch line.

Now don't get me wrong. I am not saying that the plastic in the Great Pacific Garbage Patch is no big deal. It most certainly is. In fact, that's what makes this fraud so insidious. When someone like Moore comes along and paints such an unrealistic picture of a serious problem and the media pick up on it, that picture becomes the definition of the problem. When a serious scientist like White then comes along and tells you what the problem *really* looks like, it suddenly doesn't seem very bad at all.

In the end, the Great Pacific Garbage Patch is a problem, and it is a serious problem. However, in my opinion, Moore and Ebbesmeyer have made the problem worse, because they have given people a reason to downplay it.

*"[On] certain issues—like this one—
that threaten our economy, our health
and our way of life, I do believe that
government has a responsibility to its
people and an appropriate role to play."*

Plastic Bags Are a Huge Waste Problem and Should Be Banned

Marc Basnight

Marc Basnight is a North Carolina state senator. In the following viewpoint, he states that reducing the use of plastic bags is necessary in order to protect the natural beauty of the Outer Banks in North Carolina. Basnight notes that small changes in behavior can have far-reaching effects and that individuals should be willing to sacrifice a little convenience for environmental benefits. He proposes a total ban on the use of plastic bags to protect the marine ecosystem of the Outer Banks.

As you read, consider the following questions:

1. What are plastic bags made out of, as stated in the viewpoint?

Marc Basnight, "Should the Plastic Bag Ban Be Extended to All Outer Banks Businesses?" *Island Free Press*, June 10, 2010. Reproduced by permission of the author.

2. What did Thomas Jefferson say about responsibility to the environment and frugality with resources?

3. What are the benefits of reusable bags, according to Basnight?

The Outer Banks [in North Carolina] has always been a place where the people's livelihoods depended on the bounty of our land and our waters. Even as our community has grown and changed over the centuries, our reliance on our natural resources remains the same. Our commercial watermen, who bring in fresh seafood every day, need a healthy fishery to survive. Our small businesses, recreational industry, and tourism-based economy rely on clean water and beautiful beaches. For me, as for so many others who are fortunate to call this place our home, protecting these natural gifts is not an environmental issue—it is an economic one.

That concern for the economic well-being of our community, and for the health of our people, is what led me to last year's [2009's] law to reduce the use of plastic bags in the Outer Banks. The Outer Banks is in the business of looking good. Our natural beauty is a top reason that millions of people come here every year and support our economy. I have seen so many bags in our area, as I know you have—hanging in trees, from marsh grasses, and on our dune's sea oats. They flutter along in the wind and likely end up in our waters. At some point I began to wonder what effects these plastic bags were having on our environment—or if they posed no more harm than simply being an eyesore.

The Environmental Consequences of Plastic Bags

I began to look into the issues of plastics and waste, and what I found was disturbing. In an area of the Pacific Ocean—nobody is sure of the exact size, but scientists say that it is certainly larger than our entire state—there is something called

Facts About the Plastic Bag Problem

- 500 billion to 1 trillion plastic bags are used every year, worldwide.

- About 1 million plastic bags are used every minute.

- A single plastic bag can take up to 1,000 years to degrade.

Reuseit.com,
"Facts About the Plastic Bag Pandemic," 2010.

the [Great] Pacific Garbage Patch, consisting of billions upon billions of pieces of plastic, from microscopic size to chunks as big as a lawn chair. A 1999 study found six times more plastic than plankton in water samples of the Pacific Ocean. When I heard about large concentrations of plastic debris in the Atlantic as well, I began to fear for the health and future of our fisheries here at home.

The Mayo Clinic already cautions us about fish that may be contaminated with mercury and other pollutants, and I fear that plastics could further contaminate our marine life. Plastic bags are made of high-density polyethylene and titanium chloride—or more simply put, complex carbons and transitional metal—and they break down into tiny pieces in the water. Scientists are currently studying the potential impacts these plastic materials and other chemicals could have on marine life and, later, to human health as a result of seafood consumption. And although we do not yet know for certain what these impacts will be to our fisheries, I would much rather err on the side of caution than to see our fisheries fall apart because of something that we could have stopped.

We Must Change Our Habits

Our waters have sustained our community's culture and economy for generations. And it is our future that could be in jeopardy. But if we cannot make one small change here to help prevent that, why would anyone else fight for us? Why would Washington or Raleigh [the capital of North Carolina] take steps to protect the health of our fisheries? Why would America or China or anyone else reduce carbon emissions to reduce mercury in our waters? If we do not show we are willing to make a change at home, nobody will stand up for us.

This is why I feel so strongly about reducing the presence of plastic bags on the Outer Banks. There is nothing I like about the overreaching of government. I have seen our federal government strangle our commercial fishermen, prevent our bridge from being built, and break a longtime promise to maintain public access to our national seashore. But on certain issues—like this one—that threaten our economy, our health and our way of life, I do believe that government has a responsibility to its people and an appropriate role to play.

I fully abide by our forefathers' beliefs that a person should be frugal and responsible with the materials around him. In 1806 Thomas Jefferson said, "We must use a good deal of economy in our wood, never cutting down new, where we can make the old do." Today, Jefferson and others who founded our country would urge us to use and reuse what we have, and not be wasteful—because when we cast it aside, it becomes someone else's problem. Plastic bags may be a convenience now, but what problems are we creating tomorrow through our convenience today?

Passing a More Comprehensive Law

Last year's law applied to flimsy lightweight bags sold at large major retailers. I believe it has made a difference but there is more we can do. This year, I proposed that this law be extended to apply to all businesses on the Outer Banks of Dare,

Currituck, and Hyde counties and apply to plastic bags of all weights—a total ban on plastic bags on our barrier islands. But I do not want to move forward with this law without input from you—because we all share in this community's future together, and it's only by working together that we can make the Outer Banks a better place for the future.

I have already sent a letter to more than 600 Outer Banks businesses to explain my proposal and my reasoning, and to ask for feedback and support. I have received little negative reaction thus far, but I sincerely want to hear your thoughts and concerns about the potential threat that plastics pose to our marine life and our fisheries—and to the future of our community. . . .

Banning plastic bags is not about getting you to use paper bags, or even keeping you from having plastic bags. It is not about whether or not tourists will show up with reusable bags or be annoyed by having to use paper. Rather, it is about you and me making small changes that could have a lasting effect on our community's future. Using reusable bags is easy. They are cheap to buy, easy to carry, and sturdy. They hold plenty of groceries, and are built to hold everything from a carton of eggs to nuts and bolts and tools. By making reusable bags your habit, those of us that live here can show the rest of America that it is not difficult to use reusable bags. And we can demonstrate how great our natural areas look and how our waters are free from plastic debris because of our small efforts.

| "The [New York] City Council hasn't voted to outlaw my beloved bags . . . yet."

Plastic Bags Are Useful and Should Not Be Banned

Lenore Skenazy

Lenore Skenazy was a columnist for the New York Sun, *until the newspaper ceased publication in 2008. In the following viewpoint, Skenazy maintains that the choice to ban plastic bags, as a number of local governments and corporations have done, is not as clear-cut as environmentalists make it out to be. Skenazy insists that many people not only recycle plastic bags but reuse them as often as possible, frequently as a handy and effective alternative to trash bags, and that a ban on plastic bags is not as smart as getting the most use out of them as possible and handling them in an environementally responsible way.*

As you read, consider the following questions:

1. Why does Skenazy oppose outlawing plastic bags?

2. What are some examples, given by the author, of reuse of plastic bags?

Lenore Skenazy, "Please Don't Call That Bag Garbage," *New York Sun*, October 31, 2007. www.nysun.com. Reproduced by permission.

3. Why does Skenazy maintain that plastic bags are not an "unmitigated blessing"?

You can have my plastic bags when you pry them from my cold, Gristede's-going fingers.

Oh, I know the [New York] City Council hasn't voted to outlaw my beloved bags . . . yet. On Monday [in October 2007], it simply introduced a bill that would require any largish store to ask its customers to please recycle its plastic bags. The store would then have to set up some recycling bins to actually take those bags, in all their post–roast chicken disgustingness, back.

Unnecessary Legislation

Nothing wrong with that. Who doesn't like recycling? (Or chicken?) The only thing is: If ever a city knew how to wring maximum use out of its grocery bags already, it is this one. The Inuit and their blubber this, blubber that, have nothing on New Yorkers and their bags.

"I use them to line every bathroom garbage can. I doublebag my kitty litter. I take them everywhere I go to collect snack garbage. And I always have one at the bottom of my purse," my bag-besotted friend Wendi said.

Who has not been thrilled to discover a D'Ag bag [from D'Agostino Supermarkets] just as they were trying to figure out what to do with the lunch, laundry, or dirty diaper suddenly on hand? Who has not wrapped a plastic bag around a bottle of something they didn't want to explode inside their other bag (Duane Reade, circa 1998)? Unlike their suburban counterparts, New Yorkers even use their grocery bags to take out the kitchen trash, since anything bigger is impossible to shove down the chute. (Not that I haven't tried.) "And is there not something poetic about watching a plastic bag whip across an asphalt parking lot, the urban equivalent of watching tumbleweed bounce across the prairie?" blogger Dan Collins asked.

A Tax, Not a Ban

In 2002, Ireland passed a tax on plastic bags; customers who want them must now pay 33 cents per bag at the register. There was an advertising awareness campaign. And then something happened that was bigger than the sum of these parts.

Within weeks, plastic bag use dropped 94 percent.

Elisabeth Rosenthal,
"Motivated by a Tax, Irish Spurn Plastic Bags,"
New York Times, *February 2, 2008.*

Downsides to Plastic Bags

Well . . . uh. I'm not sure I'd go that far.

The fact is, when plastic bags are not cleverly reused by brilliant and thrifty types, they can spread a certain gloom. It's hard to enthuse about a bag stuck in a tree—something South Africans call their "national flower."

Environmentalists remind us that even when bags are properly disposed of they will languish in landfills. Yet if they escape—yikes. "A bag floating in the water looks like a jellyfish, which for a lot of marine creatures means it looks like lunch," a spokesman for the Natural Resources Defense Council, Jon Coifman, said.

So, it's true: Plastic bags are not an unmitigated blessing.

Recycle, Don't Ban, Plastic Bags

That's why the City Council's pending bill seems surprisingly smart. Unlike other cities, including, most recently, San Francisco, it does not seek to ban the bags outright. Instead, it would allow New Yorkers to keep stockpiling them, if they're running low on garbage bags, or to get rid of them responsibly if they've got so many that they can't shut the kitchen cabinet anymore and their husband is hollering, "What in God's name are you saving these for?" Until now, plastic bags were not accepted as recyclables.

With a new focus on the plastic bag's ubiquity, the law may also remind us that it makes sense to carry around a tote bag, too, just like all those WNYC [public radio] supporters all those years. This is something I'd like to start doing (but not if I have to wear the shoes).

Anyway, even with a sturdy tote, I know what I'll always have tucked inside: New York's answer to whale blubber.

Periodical and Internet Sources Bibliography

The following articles have been selected to supplement the diverse views presented in this chapter.

Gloria Allen	"Legislators Off Target with 'Bag Bill,'" *Our Weekly*, August 12, 2010.
Consumer Reports	"Paper or Plastic? How About a Tote?," May 2009.
Kitt Doucette	"An Ocean of Plastic," *Rolling Stone*, October 29, 2009.
Dave Lawrence	"Plastic Particles Permeate the Atlantic," *Oceanus*, August 2010.
Dan Morain	"Bag Ban: Nice Cause, Flimsy Idea," *Sacramento Bee*, September 1, 2010.
David Pogue	"Maybe We Should Ban Paper Bags, Too," WestportNow.com, September 6, 2008. http://westportnow.com.
Nina Shen Rastogi	"Sea Trash," Slate.com, February 9, 2010. www.slate.com
John Rather	"Tapping Power from Trash," *New York Times*, September 13, 2008.
Daniel Stone	"The Great Pacific Cleanup," *Newsweek*, December 10, 2009.
Travis Williams and Gus Gates	"Banning Plastic Bags: Putting an End to Our Wasteful Habit," OregonLive.com, February 9, 2010. www.oregonlive.com.
William Yardley	"Many Plans to Curtail Use of Plastic Bags, but Not Much Action," *New York Times*, February 23, 2009.

OPPOSING
VIEWPOINTS®
SERIES

CHAPTER 2

Is Recycling Effective?

Chapter Preface

As the US recycling movement began to take root in the late 1960s and early 1970s, communities began to experiment with programs that aimed to discourage large amounts of household waste and encourage recycling, composting, and better consumer choices. One of the more popular strategies to come out of that period was pay-as-you-throw (PAYT) programs, also known as unit pricing, variable rate pricing, or user pay. First used in San Francisco as early as the mid-1930s, PAYT charges households or businesses a rate based on how much waste they put out for collection. The charge can be calculated on the weight of the garbage or the size of the load, which is stored in containers or bags. Recycling services are provided for free in order to encourage the practice.

There are three major categories of PAYT programs. For full-unit pricing, users pay in advance for their garbage by purchasing or renting a tag or container from the municipality. Partial-unit pricing involves the municipality setting a limit on the maximum number of bags or containers of garbage; if households or businesses exceed the maximum, they must pay a fee for extra bags or containers. In variable-rate pricing, users rent a container corresponding to the amount of waste they generate every collection period and are charged according to that.

In the 1970s, more municipalities began to adopt PAYT programs. Cities and towns in California, New York, Michigan, and Washington all implemented versions of the scheme. Today, thousands of communities in America rely on PAYT strategies and are credited for helping to reduce the amount of residential waste that ends up in landfills around the country.

For many environmentalists and local government officials, PAYT programs hold a strong appeal. Supporters maintain that PAYT schemes have an economic benefit, as they tend to remove a great part of the cost of waste management from property tax bills by directly charging users by the cost of consumption. PAYT also encourages more environmentally responsible behavior; if users are charged by the amount of waste they throw out, users will want to save money by adopting practices like recycling and composting. It may also force consumers to consider the amount of packaging there is in the products they purchase, hereby encouraging them to buy products that utilize less packaging. A change in such behavior would have a direct environmental impact, because it means less waste in landfills and incinerators and less resources utilized to collect waste and transport it.

Critics of PAYT programs point out that although such schemes have succeeded in some communities, they have failed in others. They also point out that charging by the bag or container leads to cheating, as users find ways to cram more garbage into smaller containers to avoid extra fees. PAYT can result in illegal dumping, as users may resort to dumping their excess waste, leading to extra costs in environmental cleanups.

The debate over PAYT programs is just one of the subjects about the value of recycling included in the following chapter. Other viewpoints examine the environmental impact of recycling, its social value, and problems incurred by implementing it in communities around the United States.

> "The extra money earned by recycling aluminum could also build over time and eventually be used for something much desired."

Recycling Reinforces Social Responsibility

Christal Marx

Christal Marx is the education program coordinator for Keep Evansville Beautiful. In the following viewpoint, she suggests that recycling teaches not only fiscal responsibility, but also other important lessons like civic pride, discipline, and social and environmental responsibility. Marx tells the story of a friend who was able to buy a new bike by recycling aluminum cans and contends that kids can still do this in tough economic times.

As you read, consider the following questions:

1. How much does Marx say a pound of aluminum is worth?

2. How old was Marx's friend, Chris Cole, when he earned a new bike by recycling?

3. How long did it take Cole to earn enough money collecting aluminum cans to buy the bike?

Christal Marx, "Recycling Teaches Important Lessons," *Evansville Courier & Press*, November 26, 2010. Reproduced by permission of the author.

'Tis the season for penny pinching, coupon clipping and door busting for discounts.

This time of year [November 2010] is always harsh on our pocketbooks.

Fortunately, there is an easy way to earn extra cash by recycling aluminum cans.

A pound of aluminum is worth about 50 cents right now. Just five pounds will return about $2.50.

As the holiday season approaches, every dollar counts.

Recycling Teaches Fiscal Responsibility

That extra $2.50 could be a large can of yams for a holiday dinner, a Christmas card for a loved one or close to a gallon of gas for holiday travel.

The extra money earned by recycling aluminum could also build over time and eventually be used for something much desired.

Years ago, a friend of mine, Evansville resident Chris Cole, did just that to earn a brand-new bike at the ripe age of 7. It can still be done today.

Chris got his first bicycle when he was 5 years old, and like most growing boys, by the age of 7 he was tall enough for his knees to touch the handlebars.

He complained to his mother about wanting a new one, and so she said what every impatient child hates hearing: "Maybe Santa will bring you one for Christmas."

Chris's grandfather heard the conversation and devised a plan to help Chris earn the bike on his own without having to wait for Santa's sleigh.

Chris's grandfather told him about the county line road near his house where people tossed their trash as they were speeding by.

He told him that it was filled with litter that no one ever bothered to pick up and there were lots of aluminum cans worth money along that stretch.

Recycling Trends

Over the last few decades, the generation, recycling, composting, and disposal of MSW [municipal solid waste] have changed substantially. While solid waste generation has increased, from 3.66 to 4.50 pounds per person per day between 1980 and 2008, the recycling rate has also increased—from less than 10 percent of MSW generated in 1980 to over 33 percent in 2008. Disposal of waste to a landfill has decreased from 89 percent of the amount generated in 1980 to 54 percent of MSW in 2008.

US Environmental Protection Agency,
"Municipal Solid Waste Generation Recycling, and Disposal
in the United States: Facts and Figures for 2008," 2009.

A Plan

So, every Friday, Saturday, and Sunday through the month of November, Chris and his grandfather would grab garbage bags and gloves and gather the trash along the littered road, mile by mile.

After four weeks of hard work, it was finally time to load up the aluminum and head to the recycling center. Chris watched the cans being dumped into heavy machinery for what felt like an hour, but was actually only about 10 minutes.

The attendant reached out to hand a pile of money to Chris's grandfather, but he pointed to Chris and said, "Actually, it's his money. He earned it."

Chris held out his hands as the man handed him $145. It was the first time he had ever seen that much money. Chris and his grandfather went to pick up the bike that had been put on layaway a month ago.

He handed the money to the cashier with a proud smile across his face. After that Chris went straight home and rode his new white Huffy down what was now a clean and can-free road.

Recycling and Social Responsibility

Chris's grandfather taught him important lessons: the value of a dollar, earning his own money, recycling, and keeping his community beautiful.

Those are all well and good, but there is something even more exciting to be said for kicking up the pegs on a brand-new bicycle before Santa Claus has even begun to load his sleigh.

| *"Recycling was always meant to be a last resort, not a free-for-all license to consume."*

Recycling Encourages Consumption and Materialism

GreenMuze.com

GreenMuze.com is an environmental website that offers the latest in green news and commentary. In the following viewpoint, the author observes that wealthy countries like the United States try to rationalize their outrageous rates of consumption through recycling. Instead, the author suggests, Americans should focus on being more conscientious and careful consumers in order to reduce their waste.

As you read, consider the following questions:

1. How much trash does the typical American produce every year, according to the viewpoint?

2. How much more trash does the viewpoint author state an average North American produces than an individual in Central America or Africa?

3. What percentage of their waste does the viewpoint author state that Americans recycled in 2005?

"Recycle: A Social Commentary," GreenMuze.com, August 25, 2008. Reproduced by permission.

When we talk about global consumption, individuals in developed nations always manage to rationalize the amount of waste they produce by insisting they recycle. It's as if, we somehow believe, recycling mitigates consumption. Unfortunately, the so-called benefits of recycling have now reached mythological proportions.

Social theorists posit that when recycling is seen as taking appropriate responsibility for excessive materialism, it might actually operate to normalize the gluttonous habits of many wealthy nations. The belief is that, in many nations, recycling allows individuals to engage in disproportionate patterns of consumption. Of course, not everyone consumes equally.

North Americans Produce More Garbage

It seems the wealthier the country, the more waste the citizens produce. Each year, the average American citizen produces 726 kilograms of trash. Canadians produce 1,000 kilograms per person. Individuals in the UK [United Kingdom] produce about half that amount—592 kilograms per person.

Americans make up only 4.6% of the population, yet they somehow manage to produce more than 40% of the world's trash. North Americans generate and throw away 9 times as much waste as an individual in Central America or Africa. Clearly, not everyone consumes equally.

Who Recycles?

Nor does everybody recycle equally either. Americans recycled about 32% of their waste in 2005. Canadians recycle about 25% of their household waste. The UK is recycling less than 18% of its waste. Steel, aluminum, paper and glass continue to be the most recycled materials on the planet, but even in countries where a solid recycling infrastructure is in place, recovery rates remain low. The barrier doesn't appear to be access to recycling facilities or lack of economic incentives for reclaiming materials, but more, a belief that we lack responsibility for the waste we produce.

Reduce, Reuse, Recycle

When environmentalists became preoccupied with consumer consumption in the early 1970s, the now familiar environmental adage—reduce, reuse, recycle (the 3Rs equation)—was formulated. The rationale behind the 3Rs was an attempt to illustrate the necessity, economically and environmentally, of obtaining the maximum benefit from products while generating the minimum amount of waste. It made sense then and it still does today.

Yet we seem to fixate on recycling today, forgetting or ignoring the importance of the reduction and reuse component of the equation. Recycling was always meant to be a last resort, not a free-for-all license to consume. We have to ask ourselves, with landfills overflowing, incinerators pouring out toxic pollution, a plastic island the size of Texas floating in the Pacific Ocean, with resources like petroleum, trees and water running low, are we willing, as a species, to literally consume ourselves to death?

We lost our way for a time. Perhaps it was the seductive presence of so many bright, shiny, cheap conveniences that made us stop taking responsibility for our consumption. Or maybe it was a malaise or fatigue, an unhappiness that drove us to seek to fill the growing emptiness inside.

It is the time to bring the 'reduce and reuse' component back into our lives. We need to practice conscientious consumption; to become more mindful of every product, service and object we consume, even if it means we literally need to ask ourselves before each purchase—*Do I really need this? Where did this object come from? How was it made? How far did it travel to get to this shop?*—then so be it. Each and every choice matters. Now more than ever.

> "In reality, the only real beneficiaries of the recycling movement are environmental groups and recycling companies."

Recycling Does Not Solve Environmental Problems

Anthony B. Bradley

Anthony B. Bradley is an associate professor of theology at the King's College in New York City and a research fellow at the Acton Institute. In the following viewpoint, he deems many of the supposed benefits of recycling as myths that are being perpetrated by an environmental movement intent on "green washing" or "greenboozling" the American public. Bradley argues that the true cost of recycling and the environmental costs are often hidden by advocates of the process, leaving Americans to believe untruths and myths about the practice.

As you read, consider the following questions:

1. According to *Progressive Investor*, how much did the recycling industry grow in annual sales from 1968 to 2008?

2. What is "downcycling"?

Anthony B. Bradley, "Greenboozled," Acton Institute, December 10, 2008. Reproduced by permission.

3. What does Bradley believe should be central to any discussion about the environment?

Being "green" is the new cool. Your family's "green Christmas" and toy purchases from Greentoys.com this season will advertise to your friends and relatives that you care about the environment. But environmentalists are balking. They say that too many companies are claiming to be green and thus are "greenwashing" everything.

The Greenwashing Trend

Greenpeace describes greenwashing as the act of misleading consumers regarding the environmental practices of a company or the environmental benefits of a product or service. The deeper irony is that greenwashing was the original tactic many environmentalists used to manipulate us into adopting practices that actually do not sustain the environment. Another term for greenwashing would be greenboozled.

One of the unintended consequences of greenwashing environmental rhetoric is that being green has turned into a fad. Marketing departments have discovered how easy it is to sell products to people who want to feel good about their consumption problem. Greenwashing works because most Americans do not think about negative spillover effects, environmental processes, long-term effects on the poor, or the economic implications of allegedly environment friendly proposals. Simply saying something is green is enough for most of us. Who cares if it's true or if it works? We are satisfied with the arbitrary labeling.

Environmentalists do not want us to believe the green claims coming from large corporations in manufacturing and energy production, but these are the same people that greenwashed us into believing that ethanol is environmentally better than gasoline, that recycling improves the environment, and many other such greenwashed untruths. Stewardship of

> # Resolving the Environmental Debate
>
> To resolve the environmental debate once and for all, experts have begun to conduct detailed life-cycle analyses on recycled goods, calculating the energy consumed from the moment they're picked up by recycling trucks until they are processed into brand-new products. When compared with the amount of energy required to send the same goods to landfills or incinerators and make new products from scratch, the results vary dramatically, depending on the material.
>
> *Alex Hutchinson, "Is Recycling Worth It?*
> *PM Investigates Its Economic and Environmental Impact,"*
> Popular Mechanics, *November 13, 2008.*

the environment is yet another area furnishing evidence that ethical integrity is critical to effective action. We need more honesty and less exaggeration.

An Example of Greenwashing

The National Ethanol Vehicle Coalition (NEVC), the nation's primary advocacy group promoting the use of E85 fuel (85 percent ethanol fuel, 15 percent gasoline) as a form of alternative transportation fuel, was positioned to greenwash us until Dr. Mark Z. Jacobson of Stanford University and other researchers revealed our ignorance. In a 2007 study, Jacobson demonstrated that ethanol is just as bad for the environment as gasoline.

Due to its ozone effects, future E85 may be a greater overall public health risk than gasoline. In fact, if we move toward the proposed E85 fuel goals, it may increase ozone-related mortality, hospitalization, and asthma by 4 percent in the United States as a whole relative to 100 percent gasoline use.

Jacobson and others have concluded with confidence only that E85 is unlikely to improve air quality over future gasoline vehicles. Unburned ethanol emissions from E85 may result in a global-scale source of acetaldehyde larger than that of direct emissions. Why then is NEVC still greenboozling the American public?

The Recycling "Greenboozle"

Perhaps the greatest greenwash of all is the mythology surrounding the environmental benefits of recycling. In reality, the only real beneficiaries of the recycling movement are environmental groups and recycling companies. According to *Progressive Investor*, from 1968 to 2008, the recycling industry grew from $4.6 billion in annual sales to roughly $236 billion.

However, William McDonough and Michael Braungart, authors of *Cradle to Cradle[: Remaking the Way We Make Things]*, employing the use of reason coupled with hard data, demonstrate that the energy, chemicals, and toxins used in the recycling process create products and environmental waste that is just as hazardous as original production. This is true in part because we do not manufacture products to be recycled at the outset. As such, the waste that is produced when putting metals, plastics, and paper through recycling processes yields no environmental gain.

As McDonough and Braungart point out, the products we think we are "recycling" are actually "downcycled"—that is, we transform the material into one of lesser quality when we recycle metals, plastics, paper, and so on. For example, paper requires extensive bleaching and other chemicals to make it white again for reuse resulting in a mixture of chemicals, pulp, and at times, toxic inks.

Why, then, does the National Recycling Coalition encourage environmentally harmful processes and recycled products that eventually end up in landfills anyway? There is nothing wrong with recycling as an industry but the public should not be fooled into believing that recycling helps the environment.

What our conversations about the environment need, on all sides, is truthfulness rooted in the recognition that good intentions do not make good policy. Truthfulness in environmentalism is a call to weigh the facts, prioritize the needs of the poor, and keep government bureaucrats from instituting policy based on greenboozling rhetoric so that we can effectively meet the needs of human welfare and responsible care for our environment.

> *"If done right, there is no doubt that recycling saves energy and raw materials, and reduces pollution. But as well as trying to recycle more, it is also important to try to recycle better."*

Recycling Benefits the Environment

The Economist

The Economist is a weekly news and international affairs publication. In the following viewpoint, the writer takes a look at recent studies that conclude that the environmental benefits from recycling outweigh the environmental costs. The writer explores sustainable packaging as a welcome innovation in recycling, viewing it as a critical step in reducing the amount of waste produced around the world. The writer also touts the gains—and potential for future gains—realized by such innovations as single-stream recycling, infrared-sorting technology, green-glass conservation, and designing products and packaging that are more easily recycled.

As you read, consider the following questions:

1. As of 2007, how much of America's garbage was recycled, according to the viewpoint?

2. According to the Waste & Resources Action Programme (WRAP) study, in what percentage of all scenarios that included recycling was it indeed better for the environment?

3. What country does the author state has become the largest importer of recyclable materials in the world?

It is an awful lot of rubbish. Since 1960 the amount of municipal waste being collected in America has nearly tripled, reaching 245m [million] tonnes in 2005. According to European Union statistics, the amount of municipal waste produced in western Europe increased by 23% between 1995 and 2003, to reach 577kg [kilograms] per person. (So much for the plan to reduce waste per person to 300kg by 2000.) As the volume of waste has increased, so have recycling efforts. In 1980 America recycled only 9.6% of its municipal rubbish; today [2007] the rate stands at 32%. A similar trend can be seen in Europe, where some countries, such as Austria and the Netherlands, now recycle 60% or more of their municipal waste. Britain's recycling rate, at 27%, is low, but it is improving fast, having nearly doubled in the past three years.

Even so, when a city introduces a kerbside recycling programme, the sight of all those recycling lorries trundling around can raise doubts about whether the collection and transportation of waste materials requires more energy than it saves. "We are constantly being asked: Is recycling worth doing on environmental grounds?" says Julian Parfitt, principal analyst at Waste & Resources Action Programme (WRAP), a nonprofit British company that encourages recycling and develops markets for recycled materials.

An Insightful Study

Studies that look at the entire life cycle of a particular material can shed light on this question in a particular case, but WRAP decided to take a broader look. It asked the Technical University of Denmark and the Danish Topic Centre on Waste [and Resources] to conduct a review of 55 life-cycle analyses, all of which were selected because of their rigorous methodology. The researchers then looked at more than 200 scenarios, comparing the impact of recycling with that of burying or burning particular types of waste material. They found that in 83% of all scenarios that included recycling, it was indeed better for the environment.

Based on this study, WRAP calculated that Britain's recycling efforts reduce its carbon-dioxide emissions by 10m–15m tonnes per year. That is equivalent to a 10% reduction in Britain's annual carbon-dioxide emissions from transport, or roughly equivalent to taking 3.5m cars off the roads. Similarly, America's Environmental Protection Agency estimates that recycling reduced the country's carbon emissions by 49m tonnes in 2005.

Recycling has many other benefits, too. It conserves natural resources. It also reduces the amount of waste that is buried or burnt, hardly ideal ways to get rid of the stuff. (Landfills take up valuable space and emit methane, a potent greenhouse gas; and although incinerators are not as polluting as they once were, they still produce noxious emissions, so people dislike having them around.) But perhaps the most valuable benefit of recycling is the saving in energy and the reduction in greenhouse gases and pollution that result when scrap materials are substituted for virgin feedstock. "If you can use recycled materials, you don't have to mine ores, cut trees and drill for oil as much," says Jeffrey Morris of Sound Resource Management, a consulting firm based in Olympia, Washington.

Extracting metals from ore, in particular, is extremely energy intensive. Recycling aluminum, for example, can reduce energy consumption by as much as 95%. Savings for other materials are lower but still substantial: about 70% for plastics, 60% for steel, 40% for paper and 30% for glass. Recycling also reduces emissions of pollutants that can cause smog, acid rain and the contamination of waterways.

A Brief History of Recycling

The virtue of recycling has been appreciated for centuries. For thousands of years metal items have been recycled by melting and reforming them into new weapons or tools. It is said that the broken pieces of the *Colossus of Rhodes*, a statue deemed one of the seven wonders of the ancient world, were recycled for scrap. During the industrial revolution, recyclers began to form businesses and later trade associations, dealing in the collection, trade and processing of metals and paper. America's Institute of Scrap Recycling Industries (ISRI), a trade association with more than 1,400 member companies, traces its roots back to one such organization founded in 1913. In the 1930s many people survived the Great Depression by peddling scraps of metal, rags and other items. In those days reuse and recycling were often economic necessities. Recycling also played an important role during the Second World War, when scrap metal was turned into weapons.

As industrial societies began to produce ever-growing quantities of garbage, recycling took on a new meaning. Rather than recycling materials for purely economic reasons, communities began to think about how to reduce the waste flow to landfills and incinerators. Around 1970 the environmental movement sparked the creation of America's first kerbside collection schemes, though it was another 20 years before such programmes really took off.

A Revolutionary Approach

In 1991 Germany made history when it passed an ordinance shifting responsibility for the entire life cycle of packaging to producers. In response, the industry created Duales System Deutschland (DSD), a company that organises a separate waste-management system that exists alongside public rubbish collection. By charging a licensing fee for its "green dot" trademark, DSD pays for the collection, sorting and recycling of packaging materials. Although the system turned out to be expensive, it has been highly influential. Many European countries later adopted their own recycling initiatives incorporating some degree of producer responsibility.

In 1987 a rubbish-laden barge cruised up and down America's East Coast looking for a place to unload, sparking a public discussion about waste management and serving as a catalyst for the country's growing recycling movement. By the early 1990s so many American cities had established recycling programmes that the resulting glut of materials caused the market price for kerbside recyclables to fall from around $50 per tonne to about $30, says Dr Morris, who has been tracking prices for recyclables in the Pacific Northwest since the mid-1980s. As with all commodities, costs for recyclables fluctuate. But the average price for kerbside materials has since slowly increased to about $90 per tonne.

Even so, most kerbside recycling programmes are not financially self-sustaining. The cost of collecting, transporting and sorting materials generally exceeds the revenues generated by selling the recyclables, and is also greater than the disposal costs. Exceptions do exist, says Dr Morris, largely near ports in dense urban areas that charge high fees for landfill disposal and enjoy good market conditions for the sale of recyclables.

Sorting Things Out

Originally kerbside programmes asked people to put paper, glass and cans into separate bins. But now the trend is toward comingled or "single stream" collection. About 700 of America's 10,000 kerbside programmes now use this approach, says Kate Krebs, executive director of America's National Recycling Coalition. But the switch can make people suspicious: If there is no longer any need to separate different materials, people may conclude that the waste is simply being buried or burned. In fact, the switch towards single-stream collection is being driven by new technologies that can identify and sort the various materials with little or no human intervention. Single-stream collection makes it more convenient for householders to recycle, and means that more materials are diverted from the waste stream.

San Francisco, which changed from multi- to single-stream collection a few years ago, now boasts a recycling rate of 69%—one of the highest in America. With the exception of garden and food waste, all the city's kerbside recyclables are sorted in a 200,000-square-foot facility that combines machines with the manpower of 155 employees. The $38m plant, next to San Francisco Bay, opened in 2003. Operated by Norcal Waste Systems, it processes an average of 750 tonnes of paper, plastic, glass and metals a day.

A Look at the Process

The process begins when a truck arrives and dumps its load of recyclables at one end of the building. The materials are then piled on to large conveyer belts that transport them to a manual sorting station. There, workers sift through everything, taking out plastic bags, large pieces of cardboard and other items that could damage or obstruct the sorting machines. Plastic bags are especially troublesome as they tend to get caught in the spinning-disk screens that send weightier materials, such as bottles and cans, down in one direction and the paper up in another.

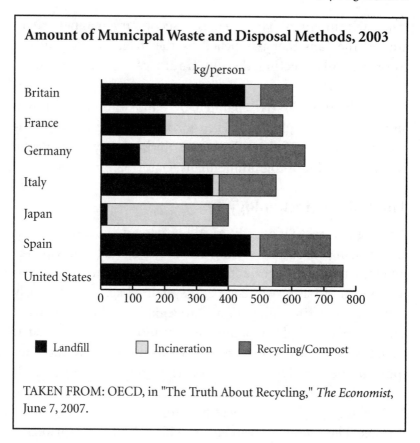

Amount of Municipal Waste and Disposal Methods, 2003

kg/person

Britain

France

Germany

Italy

Japan

Spain

United States

0   100   200   300   400   500   600   700   800

■ Landfill   □ Incineration   ■ Recycling/Compost

TAKEN FROM: OECD, in "The Truth About Recycling," *The Economist*, June 7, 2007.

Corrugated cardboard is separated from mixed paper, both of which are then baled and sold. Plastic bottles and cartons are plucked out by hand. The most common types, PET (type 1) and HDPE (type 2), are collected separately; the rest go into a mixed-plastics bin.

Next, a magnet pulls out any ferrous metals, typically tin-plated or steel cans, while the nonferrous metals, mostly aluminum cans, are ejected by eddy current. Eddy-current separators, in use since the early 1990s, consist of a rapidly revolving magnetic rotor inside a long, cylindrical drum that rotates at a slower speed. As the aluminum cans are carried over this drum by a conveyer belt, the magnetic field from the rotor induces circulating electric currents, called eddy currents, within them. This creates a secondary magnetic field around the cans that is repelled by the magnetic field of the rotor, literally ejecting the aluminum cans from the other waste materials.

Finally, the glass is separated by hand into clear, brown, amber and green glass. For each load, the entire sorting process from start to finish takes about an hour, says Bob Besso, Norcal's recycling programme manager for San Francisco.

The Role of Technology

Although all recycling facilities still employ people, investment is increasing in optical sorting technologies that can separate different types of paper and plastic. Development of the first near-infrared-based waste-sorting systems began in the early 1990s. At the time Elopak, a Norwegian producer of drink cartons made of plastic-laminated cardboard, worried that it would have to pay a considerable fee to meet its producer responsibilities in Germany and other European countries. To reduce the overall life-cycle costs associated with its products, Elopak set out to find a way to automate the sorting of its cartons. The company teamed up with SINTEF, a Norwegian research centre, and in 1996 sold its first unit in Germany. The technology was later spun off into a company now called TiTech.

TiTech's systems—more than 1,000 of which are now installed worldwide—rely on spectroscopy to identify different materials. Paper and plastic items are spread out on a conveyor belt in a single layer. When illuminated by a halogen lamp, each type of material reflects a unique combination of wavelengths in the infrared spectrum that can be identified, much like a fingerprint. By analysing data from a sensor that detects light in both the visible and the near-infrared spectrum, a computer is able to determine the colour, type, shape and position of each item. Air jets are then activated to push particular items from one conveyor belt to another, or into a bin. Numerous types of paper, plastic or combinations thereof can thus be sorted with up to 98% accuracy.

For many materials the process of turning them back into useful raw materials is straightforward: metals are shredded into pieces, paper is reduced to pulp and glass is crushed into cullet. Metals and glass can be remelted almost indefinitely without any loss in quality, while paper can be recycled up to six times. (As it goes through the process, its fibres get shorter and the quality deteriorates.)

The Question of Plastics

Plastics, which are made from fossil fuels, are somewhat different. Although they have many useful properties—they are flexible, lightweight and can be shaped into any form—there are many different types, most of which need to be processed separately. In 2005 less than 6% of the plastic from America's municipal waste stream was recovered. And of that small fraction, the only two types recycled in significant quantities were PET and HDPE. For PET, food-grade bottle-to-bottle recycling exists. But plastic is often "down-cycled" into other products such as plastic lumber (used in place of wood), drain pipes and carpet fibres, which tend to end up in landfills or incinerators at the end of their useful lives.

Even so, plastics are being used more and more, not just for packaging, but also in consumer goods such as cars, televisions and personal computers. Because such products are made of a variety of materials and can contain multiple types of plastic, metals (some of them toxic), and glass, they are especially difficult and expensive to dismantle and recycle.

Europe and Japan have initiated "take back" laws that require electronics manufacturers to recycle their products. But in America only a handful of states have passed such legislation. That has caused problems for companies that specialise in recycling plastics from complex waste streams and depend on take-back laws for getting the necessary feedstock. Michael

Biddle, the boss of MBA Polymers, says the lack of such laws is one of the reasons why his company operates only a pilot plant in America and has its main facilities in China and Austria.

Much recyclable material can be processed locally, but ever more is being shipped to developing nations, especially China. The country has a large appetite for raw materials and that includes scrap metals, waste paper and plastics, all of which can be cheaper than virgin materials. In most cases, these waste materials are recycled into consumer goods or packaging and returned to Europe and America via container ships. With its hunger for resources and the availability of cheap labour, China has become the largest importer of recyclable materials in the world.

The China Question

But the practice of shipping recyclables to China is controversial. Especially in Britain, politicians have voiced the concern that some of those exports may end up in landfills. Many experts disagree. According to Pieter van Beukering, an economist who has studied the trade of waste paper to India and waste plastics to China: "as soon as somebody is paying for the material, you bet it will be recycled."

In fact, Dr van Beukering argues that by importing waste materials, recycling firms in developing countries are able to build larger factories and achieve economies of scale, recycling materials more efficiently and at lower environmental cost. He has witnessed as much in India, he says, where dozens of inefficient, polluting paper mills near Mumbai were transformed into a smaller number of far more productive and environmentally friendly factories within a few years.

Still, compared with Western countries, factories in developing nations may be less tightly regulated, and the recycling industry is no exception. China especially has been plagued by countless illegal-waste imports, many of which are processed by poor migrants in China's coastal regions. They dismantle and recycle anything from plastic to electronic waste without any protection for themselves or the environment.

Associated Dangers of the Industry

The Chinese government has banned such practices, but migrant workers have spawned a mobile cottage industry that is difficult to wipe out, says Aya Yoshida, a researcher at Japan's National Institute for Environmental Studies who has studied Chinese waste imports and recycling practices. Because this type of industry operates largely under the radar, it is difficult to assess its overall impact. But it is clear that processing plastic and electronic waste in a crude manner releases toxic chemicals, harming people and the environment—the opposite of what recycling is supposed to achieve.

Under pressure from environmental groups, such as the Silicon Valley Toxics Coalition, some computer-makers have established rules to ensure that their products are recycled in a responsible way. Hewlett-Packard has been a leader in this and even operates its own recycling factories in California and Tennessee. Dell, which was once criticised for using prison labour to recycle its machines, now takes back its old computers for no charge. And last month [May 2007] Steve Jobs detailed Apple's plans to eliminate the use of toxic substances in its products.

Far less controversial is the recycling of glass—except, that is, in places where there is no market for it. Britain, for example, is struggling with a mountain of green glass. It is the largest importer of wine in the world, bringing in more than 1 billion litres every year, much of it in green glass bottles. But with only a tiny wine industry of its own, there is little demand for the resulting glass. Instead what is needed is clear glass, which is turned into bottles for spirits, and often exported to other countries. As a result, says Andy Dawe,

WRAP's glass technology manager, Britain is in the "peculiar situation" of having more green glass than it has production capacity for.

Britain's bottle-makers already use as much recycled green glass as they can in their furnaces to produce new bottles. So some of the surplus glass is down-cycled into construction aggregates or sand for filtration systems. But WRAP's own analysis reveals that the energy savings for both appear to be "marginal or even disadvantageous". Working with industry, WRAP has started a new programme called GlassRite Wine, in an effort to right the imbalance. Instead of being bottled at source, some wine is now imported in 24,000-litre containers and then bottled in Britain. This may dismay some wine connoisseurs, but it solves two problems, says Mr Dawe: It reduces the amount of green glass that is imported and puts what is imported to good use. It can also cut shipping costs by up to 40%.

The Future of Recycling

This is an unusual case, however. More generally, one of the biggest barriers to more efficient recycling is that most products were not designed with recycling in mind. Remedying this problem may require a complete rethinking of industrial processes, says William McDonough, an architect and the co-author of a book published in 2002 called *Cradle to Cradle: Remaking the Way We Make Things*. Along with Michael Braungart, his fellow author and a chemist, he lays out a vision for establishing "closed-loop" cycles where there is no waste. Recycling should be taken into account at the design stage, they argue, and all materials should either be able to return to the soil safely or be recycled indefinitely. This may sound like wishful thinking, but Mr McDonough has a good pedigree. Over the years he has worked with companies including Ford and Google.

An outgrowth of *Cradle to Cradle* is the Sustainable Packaging Coalition, a nonprofit working group that has developed guidelines that look beyond the traditional benchmarks of packaging design to emphasise the use of renewable, recycled and nontoxic source materials, among other things. Founded in 2003 with just nine members, the group now boasts nearly 100 members, including Target, Starbucks and Estée Lauder, some of which have already begun to change the design of their packaging.

Sustainable packaging not only benefits the environment but can also cut costs. Last year Wal-Mart, the world's biggest retailer, announced that it wanted to reduce the amount of packaging it uses by 5% by 2013, which could save the company as much as $3.4 billion and reduce carbon-dioxide emissions by 667,000 tonnes. As well as trying to reduce the amount of packaging, Wal-Mart also wants to recycle more of it. Two years ago the company began to use an unusual process, called the "sandwich bale", to collect waste material at its stores and distribution centres for recycling. It involves putting a layer of cardboard at the bottom of a rubbish compactor before filling it with waste material, and then putting another layer of cardboard on top. The compactor then produces a "sandwich" which is easier to handle and transport, says Jeff Ashby of Rocky Mountain Recycling, who invented the process for Wal-Mart. As well as avoiding disposal costs for materials it previously sent to landfill, the company now makes money by selling waste at market prices.

Innovations Will Improve Recycling Success

Evidently there is plenty of scope for further innovation in recycling. New ideas and approaches will be needed, since many communities and organisations have set high targets for recycling. Europe's packaging directive requires member states to recycle 60% of their glass and paper, 50% of metals and 22.5% of plastic packaging by the end of 2008. Earlier this year the

European Parliament voted to increase recycling rates by 2020 to 50% of municipal waste and 70% of industrial waste. Recycling rates can be boosted by charging households and businesses more if they produce more rubbish, and by reducing the frequency of rubbish collections while increasing that of recycling collections.

Meanwhile a number of cities and firms (including Wal-Mart, Toyota and Nike) have adopted zero-waste targets. This may be unrealistic but Matt Hale, director of the office of solid waste at America's Environmental Protection Agency, says it is a worthy goal and can help companies think about better ways to manage materials. It forces people to look at the entire life cycle of a product, says Dr Hale, and ask questions: Can you reduce the amount of material to begin with? Can you design the product to make recycling easier?

If done right, there is no doubt that recycling saves energy and raw materials, and reduces pollution. But as well as trying to recycle more, it is also important to try to recycle better. As technologies and materials evolve, there is room for improvement and cause for optimism. In the end, says Ms Krebs, "waste is really a design flaw."

| *"The truth . . . is that recycling is an expense, not a savings, for a city."*

Mandatory Recycling Wastes Resources

James Thayer

James Thayer is a novelist and political commentator. In the following viewpoint, Thayer argues that current laws requiring mandatory recycling are based on myths and inaccuracies that surround the financial and ecological impact of recycling on municipalities. He points out that not only does mandatory recycling waste money, it also wastes the valuable time of individuals and businesses who must sort through recyclables every week. Thayer also asserts that recycling does not save any of our natural resources.

As you read, consider the following questions:

1. According to Franklin Associates, how much more expensive is curbside recycling than conventional garbage disposal?

2. How much did a study show Seattle households spend participating in the city's mandatory curbside recycling program?

James Thayer, "Recycle This!," *Weekly Standard*, January 25, 2006. Reproduced by permission of the author.

3. According to the Nevada Policy Research Institute, where could all of America's garbage for the next millennium be put?

Elias Rohas is a garbage hauler in Seattle. He works for Rabanco/Allied Waste Industries and his beat is Magnolia, the city's tony westernmost neighborhood. According to the *Seattle Times*, Rohas has been on the job 14 years. He slowly cruises Magnolia streets, using his truck's mechanical arm to lift and dump curbside garbage bins.

Since the first of the year Rohas has enjoyed a new responsibility, one shared by Seattle policemen: He can officially determine who is breaking the law, and issue a ticket.

On January 1 [2006], placing more than 10 percent recyclable materials into a garbage bin became illegal in Seattle. An offending bin is tagged with a bright yellow slip that announces, "Recycle. It's not garbage anymore." The un-emptied bin is then left at the curb in hopes that the homeowner will learn the lesson and remove the reusable material by next week's collection. Businesses that offend three times are fined $50.

Seattle's proudly progressive leaders were alarmed when, almost two decades after voluntary recycling programs were initiated in the city—recycling rates had stalled at about 40 percent of the total amount of waste. Too many bottles and too much paper were still finding their way to the eastern Oregon landfill that receives Seattle's garbage.

So after a year-long $450,000 television, radio and newspaper education campaign, the mandatory recycling law went into effect at the first of the year. The goal is to raise the percentage of recyclables to 60 percent of total waste. Seattle is not alone, of course; many other cities, from Philadelphia to Honolulu, also have mandatory recycling programs. But these laws are based on myth and followed as faith.

Feelings but Not Facts

Recycling feels right. Echoing widespread Seattle sentiment (85 percent of the city's citizens approve of curbside recycling), the *Seattle Times* editorial board has concluded that "Recycling is a good thing." After all, using a bottle twice must be better than using it once, saving resources and sparing the landfill.

The truth, though, is that recycling is an expense, not a savings, for a city. "Every community recycling program in America today costs more than the revenue it generates," says Dr. Jay Lehr of the Heartland Institute.

A telling indicator is that cities often try to dump recycling programs when budgets are tight. As Angela Logomasini, director of risk and environmental policy at the Competitive Enterprise Institute, points out in the *Wall Street Journal*, every New York City mayor has attempted to stop the city's recycling program since it was begun in 1989. Mayor David Dinkins tried, but changed his mind when met with noisy criticism. Rudy Giuliani tried, but was sued by the Natural Resources Defense Council, which won the case. Mayor [Michael] Bloomberg has proposed temporarily ending the recycling program because, as Logomasini notes, it costs $240 per ton to recycle and only $130 per ton to send the material to a landfill. The numbers for other areas are roughly comparable. The net per-ton cost of recycling exceeds $180 in Rhode Island, while conventional garbage collection and disposal costs $120 to $160 per ton.

The funds go for trucks and collectors and inspectors and bureaucrats. Clemson professor Daniel K. Benjamin points out that Los Angeles has 800 trucks working the neighborhoods, instead of 400, due to recycling. Radley Balko at aBetterEarth.org, a project of the Institute for Humane Studies at George Mason University, writes, "That means extra wear and tear on city streets, double the exhaust emissions into the atmosphere, double the man-hours required for someone to drive and man those trucks, and double the costs of mainte-

'Typical...You don't see one for weeks then they all arrive together.'

"Typical . . . you don't see one for weeks, then they all arrive together," cartoon by Mike Mosedale. www.CartoonStock.com. Copyright © Mike Mosedale. Reproduction rights obtainable from www.CartoonStock.com.

nance and upkeep of the trucks." Jerry Taylor of the Cato Institute says costs include "the energy necessary to deliver the recyclables to the collection centers, process the post-consumer material into usable commodities for manufacturers, and deliver the processed post-consumer material to manufacturing plants." Franklin Associates, which provides consulting services for solid waste management, estimates that curbside recycling is 55 percent more expensive, pound for pound, than conventional garbage disposal.

A Waste of Your Time

City budgets aren't the only victims of recycling. Citizens also have a significant cost—their time. Seattle Public Utilities researchers (in collaboration with University of California, Davis) conducted a survey in 2005 that indicated 98 percent of Seattle households participate in the curbside recycling program, and that 16 minutes are spent recycling per household. The city contains 260,000 households, which means each week Seattleites spend almost 8,500 work days recycling. Working days lost in traffic jams are commonly cited by proponents of HOV lanes, bike paths, and light rail. Nary a word is heard about lost time when the topic is recycling.

And what are those 16 minutes spent doing? Sorting, extracting, rinsing, bundling, and stomping. In Seattle, household batteries can be put into the garbage, but not rechargeable batteries. Plastic soda bottles can be recycled, but not plastic flower pots. Plastic shopping bags go into the recycle bin (bundle them first), but not plastic produce bags or plastic freezer wrap bags. Plastic cottage cheese tubs, yes, but not plastic six-pack rings. Frozen food boxes go into the recycle bin, but not paper plates. Cardboard, sure, but not if a pizza came in it, and make sure to flatten the box. And remove any tape. Cereal boxes, yes, but pull out the liner. Typing paper, of course, but sort out the paper punch holes, as those little dots can't be recycled. Hardback books, okay, but wrestle off the covers. Metal hangers, yes: aluminum foil, no. Tin cans, you bet, but rinse them, and push the lid down into the can. No loose lids can go in the recycle bin. And no confetti.

So at least it's a fun 16 minutes. There are out-of-pocket expenses, too: Rod Kauffman, president of the Building Owners and Managers Association of Seattle and King County, says this sorting will add 10 percent to a building's janitorial bills.

Landfills Can Handle Our Waste

If we weren't recycling, wouldn't the landfills soon overflow? Al Gore certainly thinks so, as he claimed we are "running out of ways to dispose of our waste in a manner that keeps it out of either sight or mind." Nonsense. Clemson professor Daniel K. Benjamin notes that rather than running out of space, overall capacity is growing. "In fact," he says, "the United

States today has more landfill capacity than ever before." He adds that the total land area required to contain every scrap of this country's garbage for the next 100 years would be only 10 miles square. The Nevada Policy Research Institute's numbers are even more dramatic: An area 44 miles square and 120 feet deep would handle all of America's garbage for the next millennium.

America's image of landfills was fixed decades ago, and is that of Staten Island's Fresh Kills, a vast swampy expanse of detritus, with huge Caterpillar tractors trundling over it, and clouds of seagulls obscuring everything above ground. Fresh Kills received New York's garbage for 53 years before it was closed in 2001. Modern landfills have nothing in common with the place. Benjamin says that new landfills are located far from groundwater supplies, and are built on thick clay beds that are covered with plastic liners, on top of which goes another layer of sand or gravel. Pipes remove leachate, which is then treated at wastewater plants. Escaping gas is burned or sold. A park or golf course or industrial development eventually goes over the landfill.

Fresh Kills also looked dangerous, a veritable soup of deadly poisons and nasty chemicals, seeping and dissolving and dispersing. But that's not the case with new landfills. Daniel Benjamin writes, "According to the EPA's [Environmental Protection Agency's] own estimates, modern landfills can be expected to cause 5.7 cancer-related deaths over the next 300 years—just one death every 50 years. To put this in perspective, cancer kills over 560,000 people every year in the United States."

The Status of Our Resources

But what about saving precious resources by recycling? Almost 90 percent of this country's paper comes from renewable forests, and to say we will someday run out of trees is the same as saying we will some day run out of corn. According to Jerry

Taylor, we are growing 22 million acres of new forest each year, and we harvest 15 million acres, for a net annual gain of 7 million acres. The United States has almost four times more forested land today than it did 80 years ago.

Are we running out of that other staple of recycle bins, glass? All those wine and beer bottles are manufactured from silica dioxide, the fancy term for sand, which Jay Lehr points out is the most abundant mineral in the earth's crust.

Nor will we ever suffer a shortage of plastic, which is made from petroleum by-products. Today more petroleum reserves are being discovered than are being used up. And plastics can now also be synthesized from farm products. Lehr concludes, "We are not running out of, nor will we ever run out of, any of the resources we recycle."

Why then do we go to all this trouble for so little—or no—reward? Lehr says it's because "we get a warm and fuzzy feeling when we recycle." Richard Sandbrook who was executive director of the International Institute for Environment and Development, said, "Environmentalists refuse to countenance any argument which undermines their sacred cow."

The *Seattle Times* concludes, "Recycling is almost a religion in Seattle." An irrational religion, says Professor Frank Ackerman, who specializes in environment policy at Tufts University. But his arguments cut little weight here in the Northwest. We attend the church of recycling, where perfervid faith compensates for lack of factual support.

Seattle Public Utilities estimates that 1 in 10 garbage bins will contain too much recyclable material, and so will be left full on the curb. Hauler Elias Rohas said they aren't hard to spot. "We can tell right away," he told the *Times*. He said the sound of glass is unmistakable, and that paper adds bulk without weight. "You can tell even when it's in the bag."

> *"[Removing] recyclable material from garbage will extend the life of the county's ... landfill, keeping the county's landfill rates—already the lowest in the state—cheap."*

Mandatory Recycling Helps Reduce Waste

Chris Bristol

Chris Bristol is a staff writer for the Yakima Herald-Republic. *In the following viewpoint, he reports that officials in Yakima County, Washington State, are considering a county-wide mandatory recycling program in order to extend the life of the county's landfill—and because it is the right thing to do. Bristol observes that county officials are concerned about the cultural change that such a program would entail, but they realize that it would significantly reduce waste going to the landfill.*

As you read, consider the following questions:

1. According to a 2003 study, what percentage of the material being dumped daily at the Terrace Heights landfill was easy-to-recycle paper, plastics and metal?

2. When is the county's landfill set to max out, according to Bristol?

3. What does Councilman Dave Edler feel is an obstacle to any mandatory recycling program?

R ecycling has been slow to catch on in Yakima [Washington State], and the term "mandatory recycling" is even less popular.

But Yakima County officials say the time has come to explore a countywide recycling strategy that would require cultural change on the part of political leaders and residents.

Here's why: Removing recyclable material from garbage will extend the life of the county's Terrace Heights landfill, keeping the county's landfill rates—already the lowest in the state—cheap.

Doing the Right Thing

But, adds Yakima County Commissioner Mike Leita, recycling is more than that.

"It is the right thing to do," he says. "We are being very wasteful by dumping (recyclable material) into the landfill."

No community in the Yakima Valley or central Washington, including the Tri-Cities, has mandatory recycling. Most have nothing other than drop-off bins, if that.

A private company, Yakima Waste Systems, offers a convenient curbside service for $6.50 a month, but only in the Yakima area. The service includes a large blue and gray bin on wheels similar to a garbage can, and there's no need to separate material.

Recycled paper is an especially important commodity locally and is used by Michelsen Packaging to make tray liners and other packaging for the fruit industry.

Finally Addressing the Issue of Recycling

In a recent interview, Leita said county officials are exploring a countywide recycling strategy to not only hold down landfill costs, but also to prepare for the strong possibility that state lawmakers will someday mandate recycling programs.

He said recycling has not been on the front burner because more immediate problems—budget cuts, jail contracts and regulations on storm and groundwater—are higher priorities.

But recycling is on the agenda, he added.

A 2003 study estimated that close to 40 percent of the material being dumped daily at the Terrace Heights landfill was easy-to-recycle paper, plastics and metal.

With the landfill currently set to max out in 2019, county officials say the fee to dump at $30.89 per ton—the state average is somewhere between $65 to $70 a ton—will go up when garbage has to be trucked to the county's Cheyne landfill near Zillah.

Leadership Is Key

The biggest users of the Terrace Heights landfill are the city of Yakima and Yakima Waste Systems which, in addition to the curbside recycling service, also picks up garbage in suburban areas of the city.

Although he stopped short of calling for anything mandatory, Leita made it clear that county officials would like local municipalities, particularly Yakima, to start recycling.

"We control the landfill," he said. "I suppose I could say we have the authority to say if you don't recycle you can't dump here, go find your own landfill. But we're good guys. . . .

"Bottom line, we would welcome any city, especially the city of Yakima, to initiate recycling efforts. There's nothing preventing them from doing that, except leadership."

The Political Dynamics of Recycling

In Yakima City Councilman Dave Edler, Leita has a key political ally. As a member of the council's Economic Development

Committee, he is aware of the county's stance on the Terrace Heights landfill and the effect space may play on county policy.

He said he would like city staff to explore the possibility of a mandatory recycling program in the form of a private-public partnership with Yakima Waste Systems.

"It's a fishing expedition, I guess," he said. "Pushing for what I would call cultural change. That comes hard around here."

Resistance to change would include some of his colleagues on the City Council, noting that then Councilman Ron Bonlender "got shot down" when he brought up the subject several years ago.

"I'm not sure how it will go, especially with the council we have, but I'm not opposed to creating a conversation, that's all."

Exploring the Logistics of Recycling

Scott Robertson, manager of Yakima Waste Systems, said he has yet to hear from city officials about the possibility of a partnership. The city has its own garbage service, which it might be wary of undercutting.

Robertson said the company's fee of $6.50 per month, billed in $13 installments every other month, would go down if the service was more widespread or if the city instituted a mandatory program.

"We'd be happy to provide it to the whole city if that's where they want to go," he said.

Leita, meanwhile, agreed with Edler that mandatory recycling would require a political buy-in that so far the region lacks.

A Possible Campaign Issue

The subject could become a campaign issue if Yakima voters approve a strong-mayor proposal in next month's [February 2011's] special election. Both men are considered frontrunners for the job, though neither has publicly expressed an interest in being the first mayor.

"Diverting recyclable material from garbage generates significant savings for the landfill," Leita said, but "It's also about doing the right thing."

Edler agreed.

"Even in a conservative community," adds Edler, "we have a responsibility to take care of our environment."

> *"The Orwellian intrusion into the lives of peaceful Britons is justified primarily on the same grounds used by Cleveland: It is a 'green' measure to preserve the environment."*

Mandatory Recycling Undermines Civil Liberties

Wendy McElroy

Wendy McElroy is an author, social and political commentator, and blogger. In the following viewpoint, she laments the implementation of a mandatory recycling scheme in Cleveland, Ohio, noting it is based on a British program that uses tiny microchips to monitor trash and recycling. McElroy considers mandatory recycling programs as an example of intrusive government control over private citizens' activities. She claims that people's privacy rights are being violated with such programs more out of a desire to raise municipal revenue than to protect the environment.

As you read, consider the following questions:

1. How many Cleveland households will be taking part in the mandatory recycling program with RFID technology in 2011, according to McElroy?

Wendy McElroy, "Big Brother Is Watching You Recycle," *The Freeman*, December 1, 2010. Reproduced by permission. www.TheFreemanOnline.org.

2. How many Britons does the viewpoint state have RFID bins?

3. According to Cleveland waste-collection commissioner Ronnie Owens, how many citations did the city expect to issue for noncompliance in 2010?

In 2009, after four years of controversial and piecemeal policies intended to enforce recycling, England imposed a complex and compulsory system of garbage-sorting on home owners.

Citing the British model, Cleveland, Ohio, is taking a giant step toward a similar scheme of compulsory recycling. In 2011 some 25,000 households will be required to use recycling bins fitted with radio-frequency identification tags (RFIDs)—tiny computer chips that can remotely provide information such as the weight of the bin's contents and that allow passing garbage trucks to verify their presence. If a household does not put its recycle bin out on the curb, an inspector could check its garbage for improperly discarded recyclables and fine the scofflaws $100. Moreover, if a bin is put out in a tardy manner or left out too long, the household could be fined. Cleveland plans to implement the system citywide within six years.

Extreme recycling programs are nothing new, even in American cities. In San Francisco recycling and composting are mandatory; trash is sorted into three different bins with compliance enforced through fines.

Neither are RFID bins new. They were introduced on London streets in 2005 ostensibly to track the amount of trash households produced and to discourage "overproduction," but they have also had trials in American cities. Earlier this year [2010], Alexandria, Virginia, approved such bins, which should be placed with households this autumn.

The Case of Cleveland

Cleveland is particularly important, however, because of its size. Cash-starved local governments will be watching to see if

RFID Technology

Radio-frequency identification (RFID) is a generic term that is used to describe a system that transmits the identity (in the form of a unique serial number) of an object or person wirelessly, using radio waves. It's grouped under the broad category of automatic identification technologies.

Association for Automatic Identification and Mobility,
"What Is RFID?," 2010.

an American city as big as Cleveland can use RFID bins to increase revenues. The revenues would flow from three basic sources: a trash-collection fee that could be increased, as in Alexandria; the imposition of fines; and the profit, if any, from selling recyclables. The latter source should not be dismissed. Recycling programs are not generally cost efficient, but much of the reason is that collections need to be cleaned and re-sorted at their destination. If households can be forced to assume these labor-intensive tasks, then selling recyclables is more likely to be profitable, especially such goods as aluminum cans. (Perversely, the demand for volume recycling may hit the poor the hardest; in the wake of recession, it has become increasingly common for people to hoard their aluminum cans in order to turn them in for cash.)

The British Model

Since the British system is praised as a role model, it is useful to examine its specifics.

An estimated 2.6 million Britons now have RFID bins monitoring how and when they sort garbage from recyclables. Implementation varies from borough to borough since trash collection, as in America, is under local jurisdiction. But the basics of the scheme are the same, with fines for noncompliance ranging up to 1,000 pounds (over $1,500).

Councils routinely employ "rubbish police," who fine households that commit offenses such as producing "excessive" trash. For example, Oxford employs "waste education officers" who go through household bins and instruct the owners on proper sorting and disposal; the officers also fine residents 80 pounds if the trash overflows the 240-liter bin, which is emptied fortnightly. Of course, this makes trash from a large party or other events like Christmas problematic. (Such a fine differs from a fee for additional service in at least two ways. The "customer" is unable to cancel the service and go to a competitor, and the fine is absurdly high, especially given the extremely low service provided.)

The policing of trash bins is also enforced by surveillance cameras; this practice became evident in a recent controversy when a Coventry woman was captured on video throwing a cat in a trash bin.

The British system also mandates how trash is to be sorted. The U.K. [United Kingdom] website Green Launches explained gleefully:

> The next time you dump your garbage in a bin, make sure you have it sorted well and dropped in the correct bin. Or else, you'll probably burn a £1,000 fine in your pocket. Household waste like food scraps, tea bags, etc., in the wrong bin will have the family penalized. This forces families to use up to five different types of bins for waste separation and encourages picking up of recyclable products. This will also include the compulsory use of slop buckets to get rid of food waste.

Cleveland is not suggesting such an elaborate division of trash. But neither did Britain initially. Government control tends to expand, and rapidly so, if the policies being imposed raise revenue.

Go Green, Rake in Revenue

The Orwellian [similar to the totalitarian government depicted in George Orwell's novel *Nineteen Eighty-Four*] intrusion into the lives of peaceful Britons is justified primarily on the same grounds used by Cleveland: It is a "green" measure to preserve the environment. Green Launches continued, "Environment secretary, Hilary Benn came up with this idea that will help reduce greenhouse gas emissions. These strict and hefty rules are sure to raise a cry amongst taxpayers and residents. But these rules will also help increase the production and use of greener energy resources and at the same time, decrease those mounting piles in landfills."

Cleveland echoes the environmental justification.

The British also justify the draconian trash system on financial grounds. Benn once exclaimed to the press, "What sort of a society would throw away aluminum cans worth £500 a ton when producers are crying out for the raw material?" Generally speaking, however, the Brits downplay the government's financial motives.

Here Cleveland parts company with its British counterparts and makes it abundantly clear that money is a driving factor. City waste-collection commissioner Ronnie Owens, who perhaps remembers the municipal bankruptcy of the 1980s, says, "The Division of Waste Collection is on track to meet its goal of issuing 4,000 citations this year [2010]." In short the goal is revenue enhancement not perfect compliance. Indeed, the two stand in conflict with each other. Bloggers have widely speculated that the recycling scheme is an excuse to create noncompliance and thus maximize the payment of fines.

Hope for Failure

Bankrupt cities across North America will be watching the Cleveland experiment. At the first indication of success—that is, of revenue enhancement—debates on mandatory recycling will break out in a multitude of city council chambers. It is not enough to hope that the Cleveland experiment will be a debacle; it almost certainly will be one but, nonetheless, debacles are often profitable to those who conduct them.

Perhaps, unlike the British, Americans will object to an RFID chip monitoring their garbage on privacy grounds. This objection may well be valid but it does not touch on the motives of local governments that consider mandatory recycling schemes. Nevertheless, it may well be the strongest defense that can be mounted.

| *"Our wallets are closer to our hearts than our recycle bins."*

Pay-As-You-Throw Programs Work

Raphael Gang and Scot Matayoshi

Raphael Gang and Scot Matayoshi are educators. In the following viewpoint, they maintain that waste disposal schemes that charge a household for the amount of trash they throw away, known as pay-as-you-throw strategies, are beneficial because they force people to think about their consumption, recycling, and waste. Gang and Matayoshi believe that such a program would result in greater recycling, composting, and conservation in their home state of Hawaii. They also argue that the resulting reductions in waste would decrease the need for landfills and that the programs offer a simple and fair way of placing greater financial burdens on individuals who create excessive waste.

As you read, consider the following questions:

1. As of 2008, how much has the amount of plastic bag waste been reduced in Ireland, according to the authors?

2. What is the tax in Ireland on a plastic bag, as reported in the viewpoint?

Raphael Gang and Scot Matayoshi, "Pay-As-You-Throw Would Change Our Habits," *Honolulu Advertiser*, February 28, 2008. Reproduced by permission of the authors.

3. According to the authors, what reason do individuals and families in Hawaii have to conserve or recycle?

Before 2002, Ireland, like the rest of the world, produced large quantities of waste in the form of plastic grocery bags. Today, the amount of plastic bag waste has been reduced by 94 percent. How did such a miracle occur? The government must have launched a massive educational campaign and spent millions of dollars teaching its citizens about the costs of their buying habits. If not that then the government must have passed a complicated regulation stating when stores are allowed to pass out plastic trash bags.

Wrong.

The Irish government imposed a 33-cent tax on every plastic bag given out in supermarkets. Most shoppers now bring their own reusable cloth bags. While this drastic change in consumer behavior may appear to be a miracle to some, it is only one example of what happens when people are forced to pay for their behavior, be it good or bad.

Hit People in the Pocketbook

Taxing something, as demonstrated by Ireland, is one of the easiest ways of either encouraging or discouraging behavior. If you want people to do more of something, tax it less (or not at all); if you want people to do less of something, tax it more.

Imagine going to the supermarket and paying only $20, no matter how much food you purchase. What would happen? People would most likely take as much food as they could carry every time they went into the market, regardless of whether or not they really needed it. This is exactly what plays out in the trash collection system in Hawai'i and many other parts of the world.

Right now, individuals and families in Hawai'i have no reason to conserve or recycle. While individuals pay a tax for their trash collection, the tax is a flat rate that encourages people to create as much trash as they want with no thought toward recycling, composting or purchasing goods with less packaging.

If I dedicate myself to reducing the amount of waste I produce, the cost of my trash collection does not go down. Likewise, if I decide to have a Super Bowl party every weekend at my house and use only paper plates and cups, I am not charged anything extra for my excessive amount of trash.

People across the board are producing more trash than they normally would, simply because they are not aware of all the costs associated with their actions.

The Cost of Trash

Running a landfill requires a lot of manpower and resources. These costs are invisible to everyone except for those operating the landfill. The Waimanalo Gulch landfill in Nanakuli is full to capacity and we are still dumping trash by the truckload. No other part of the island has to deal with the trash they create and so no one thinks twice about throwing away bottles, cans or anything else. We put it in the trash can and forget about it. What people need is a reminder of how much they threw away in the form of a bill from the city at the end of each month.

If the state and its residents are concerned about recycling and reducing the consumption of materials that cannot be recycled, how about taxing the amount of trash thrown away?

This idea is commonly referred to as a "pay as you throw" system. Communities on the Mainland and in Europe have instituted programs based on the basic premise that people should pay for the amount of trash they are producing. Individuals are charged a set rate on each bag or charged based on the weight of their trash. By showing people that there is an actual cost associated with their consumption habits, a pay-as-you-throw system encourages people to recycle, compost or

Pay-As-You-Throw Waste Strategies

In communities with pay-as-you-throw programs (also known as unit pricing or variable-rate pricing), residents are charged for the collection of municipal solid waste—ordinary household trash—based on the amount they throw away. This creates a direct economic incentive to recycle more and to generate less waste.

Traditionally, residents pay for waste collection through property taxes or a fixed fee, regardless of how much—or how little—trash they generate. Pay-As-You-Throw (PAYT) breaks with tradition by treating trash services just like electricity, gas, and other utilities. Households pay a variable rate depending on the amount of service they use.

Most communities with PAYT charge residents a fee for each bag or can of waste they generate. In a small number of communities, residents are billed based on the weight of their trash. Either way, these programs are simple and fair. The less individuals throw away, the less they pay.

US Environmental Protection Agency,
"Pay-As-You-Throw," 2011.

buy goods that have less packaging. Our wallets are closer to our hearts than our recycle bins.

Although such an idea would require planning and well-thought-out enforcement, the basic idea makes a great deal of sense.

Benefits of Pay-As-You-Throw

Imagine a world in which conserving and reducing our environmental footprint actually reaps tangible rewards.

I believe we would see a large increase in the amount of recycling, composting and conservation efforts both individually and collectively.

People would become aware of their habits and begin to save money as their trashing habits changed.

Local landfills would see large reductions in the amount of trash they handle, which would reduce the need for new landfills that would inevitably be in someone's backyard. Most importantly, an issue of basic fairness, pay for how much trash you create, would be settled in a simple and straightforward way.

> *"[Pay-as-you-throw] programs are nothing more than creative cost-shifting measures for lazy community officials to avoid dealing with their own trash disposal challenges."*

Pay-As-You-Throw Programs Do Not Work

Richard Olson Jr.

Richard Olson Jr. is a contributor to the NH Insider. In the following viewpoint, he points out that pay-as-you-throw (PAYT) programs fail to reduce the amount of trash a household produces, and they only shift the costs because households find a way to get rid of the trash and avoid higher rates. Olson argues that any cost-benefit analyses will have to include the costs of illegal dumping, as well as costs associated with this practice, in order to get an accurate view of just how much PAYT programs will cost a community. Olson's contention is that the utility of PAYT programs is limited to only a few, specific situations and does not present a viable alternative for most communities.

Richard Olson Jr., "Pay As You Throw Programs: A Contemporary Sham," *NH Insider*, September 4, 2010. Reproduced by permission of the author.

As you read, consider the following questions:

1. According to Skumatz Economic Research Associates, how much will PAYT programs reduce the flow of residential waste to incinerators and landfills?

2. What is the Seattle Stomp, as described in the viewpoint?

3. What does Olson indicate are some of the ancillary costs associated with PAYT programs?

"Pay-As-You-Throw," [PAYT] programs have enjoyed nominal success in some communities but have otherwise been an abysmal failure in others. Proponents and advocates of PAYT dismiss the contention that PAYT will fail in some communities. Oftentimes, PAYT programs are nothing more than creative cost-shifting measures for lazy community officials to avoid dealing with their own trash disposal challenge. Nevertheless, there is one constant in all PAYT programs ... great pains are taken to conceal the negative externalities of these programs. From the EPA [Environmental Protection Agency] right down to the local city government official, more often than not, the "paid trash hack" will not be candid.

Supporters always tell us PAYT gives residents an economic incentive to recycle. Skumatz Economic Research Associates, a waste-consulting firm in Superior, Colo., estimates that PAYT programs lead to a 17% reduction in the flow of residential waste to incinerators and landfills. . . . "Every analysis shows that this is a very cost-effective thing to do," says Lisa Skumatz, the firm's principal. That is not really true, though. The cost *shifts*, not reduces.

While households might reduce the number of bags, they typically do not necessarily reduce the actual weight of their household garbage. By employing the old, "Seattle Stomp," residents will reduce their garbage costs. The weight of recy-

Concerns About Illegal Dumping

The key is to design a unit pricing program that significantly deters illegal dumping and burning. Public education and enforcement policies are the most effective tools in addressing this barrier. Informing residents of the experiences of communities with unit pricing and setting up fair but aggressive enforcement policies to respond to incidents of illegal dumping also are essential.

US Environmental Protection Agency,
"Building Consensus and Planning for Unit Pricing," 2010.

cling, only nominally increases because many were already participating in voluntary recycling programs before PAYT began. Increased illegal dumping now becomes an issue, not only for the PAYT-employing community, but also for the other communities that surround it.

Strategies Used Under PAYT

The Seattle Stomp. The practice of compacting or "stomping" on ones trash in pay-as-you-throw communities, to increase the volume of garbage in a single bag so as to decrease the number of bags one must pay for to dispose of. The Seattle Stomp was so-named because Seattle, Washington, was one of the nation's first communities to implement a pay-as-you-throw program and Seattle residents responded to an early unit-pricing program by compacting garbage into fewer bags. This happens in *every* community that implements PAYT without exception.

Illegal dumping. When Charlottesville, Virginia, began charging eighty cents per 32-gallon bag of residential garbage collected at the curb, it should come as no surprise that people responded to PAYT prices as they do all other prices: they do or consume less of it. A marked increase in trash burning and illegal dumping took place.

Disproportionality. Others argue that PAYT programs wrongly penalize large families, some elderly and families with infants. A large family with three or more children will have a significantly higher trash cost than other families in other communities. Families with newborn infants will often have higher trash costs because of disposable diapers. Finally, PAYT programs often significantly affect the elderly on a fixed income where they must sometimes go without one essential item to have another.

Ancillary Costs. How much does it cost to send out a truck of municipal workers to various remote sites around a city, to pick up illegally dumped trash? How much does it cost a property owner to clean up his or her property when people illegally dump? How much time and energy will a property owner spend cleaning up after tenants who refuse to make PAYT a priority in the household expenses? How much cost will a business using dumpsters incur by increases caused by illegal use? Illegal dumpster use is already a problem in many communities that do not have PAYT. Churches, grocery stores, restaurants, and hospitals are often targets of illegal dumpster use. What about parks? Park maintenance will see a spike in costs as workers will be forced to empty trash receptacles used by those who seek to evade PAYT. PAYT [facilitators] don't include these costs in their promotion of PAYT programs.

The Concord Situation

Shortly after Concord initiated its own pay-as-you-throw program, bag sales plummeted, causing a revenue shortfall. Officials budgeted $1.95 million in bag sales but only took in $1.42 million, according to a May 22, 2010, *Concord Monitor* story. General Services Director Chip Chesley, while being vague, touted this as a "success." Such "successes" are the dishonesty of PAYT programs.

"The community response changed much faster than we thought it was going to change," Chesley tells the *Monitor*. Chesley alludes to people complying with the program citing marked increases in recycling. However, I would bet a steak dinner that a significant amount of diversion takes place in Concord and business owners from Concord and surrounding communities are noticing the effects.

PAYT was a non-issue in Bow last year when, according to the *Union Leader*, voters said "no" at a town meeting. Bow Town Manager Jim Pitts tells the [*Union Leader*], the most common argument against the program was that some residents felt they would end up paying more under pay-as-you-throw than they currently were through taxes. In many respects, the residents are correct.

The Hopkinton Situation

Hopkinton's recently adopted PAYT program was put into doubt when the town's largest trash hauler, G. Dockham Trucking, decided not to participate in the program. Dockham lost twenty-four customers the first week because the residents did not want to pay for trash bags. Ultimately, those in charge in Hopkinton will shove this program down the throats of residents, no matter who is injured by it.

PAYT programs only work in a limited variety of circumstances and communities. PAYT is no standard-bearer for efficient waste disposal and reduction of landfills. The incremental benefit of trash unit pricing is small; the social benefit does not cover the administrative cost.

Remember, when people throw something, "away," there is no "away." Garbage goes somewhere or ends up somewhere else . . . not simply, "away." PAYT merely shifts responsibility and costs to others and negative externalities are rarely reflected in PAYT analyses. There exists this circus clown–like false notion that PAYT fees collected result in a tax reduction. (A knee-slapper, if there ever was one.)

Periodical and Internet Sources Bibliography

The following articles have been selected to supplement the diverse views presented in this chapter.

Anthony DePalma — "In Economic Terms, Recycling Almost Pays," *New York Times*, May 29, 2008.

Frederick News-Post — "Recycle . . . Or Else," November 3, 2010.

Gaston Gazette — "Pay-As-You-Go Trash Collection Should Mean Less Taxes," February 10, 2011.

Alex Hutchinson — "Is Recycling Worth It? PM Investigates Its Economic and Environmental Impact," *Popular Mechanics*, November 13, 2008.

Jeff Jacoby — "The Waste of Recycling," *Patriot Post*, September 23, 2010.

E. Thomas McClanahan — "Why Bother Recycling When Landfills Are Cheaper?," *Kansas City Star*, October 30, 2010.

Iain Murray — "Time to Recycle Recycling?," *Washington Times*, June 16, 2008.

Matt Richtel and Kate Galbraith — "Back at Junk Value, Recyclables Are Piling Up," *New York Times*, December 7, 2008.

Elisabeth Rosenthal — "Business of Green: 'Pay As You Throw' Trash Disposal Catches On," *New York Times*, August 29, 2007.

Neil Seldman — "Recycling Is Not Garbage," *E Magazine*, February 11, 2008.

Christina Sloan — "The Economics of Recycling in Grand County," *Moab Times-Independent*, 2009.

Robert Tomsho — "Kicking the Cans," *Wall Street Journal*, July 29, 2008.

CHAPTER 3

Is Toxic Waste Disposal a Serious Problem?

Chapter Preface

The United States is addicted to electronic devices. Today, the majority of American households have two or more televisions, and 66 percent of American homes have more than three televisions. In 2010 more than 70 million computers were sold in the country, and nearly 293 million people own cell phones. With technological advances, state-of-the-art consumer electronics quickly become old or obsolete, motivating tech-savvy Americans to go in search of the newest model. This constant cycle of upgrading and discarding leads to an environmental quandary: What should happen to all those old and unwanted cell phones, computers, televisions, monitors, keyboards, and fax machines?

E-waste, or waste that is made up of discarded electronic devices, is becoming a rapidly increasing problem all over the world. Much of it ends up in landfills. Recent studies suggest that e-waste makes up almost 2 percent of the municipal waste stream. There are environmental problems with leaving e-waste to deteriorate in landfills; the central issue is that many electronic products contain toxic elements that will leach out into the soil and water supply. For example, mercury, arsenic, antimony trioxide, and chromium are found in many electronics. Lead is a component of cathode ray tubes. Selenium and cadmium make up many circuit boards.

To safely dispose of the exploding number of electronic products being purchased by American consumers, communities have considered various strategies. Electronic recycling, or e-cycling, is by far the most popular of these schemes. E-cycling refers to the process of collecting, brokering, taking apart, repairing, or recycling the components or metals contained in used or discarded electronic equipment.

In 2003 California passed the Electronic Waste Recycling Act to address the problem of e-waste. The law imposes a tax on certain types of electronics that the state then pays to recycling firms to recycle those products. In Europe, manufacturers are responsible for safe and efficient e-cycling efforts. In most American communities, however, e-cycling is organized by community activists or local officials.

There are many criticisms about e-cycling programs in the United States. Some commentators note that e-waste is a small percentage of overall waste and that the resources required to widely and effectively implement e-cycling programs are so expensive that the effort is not worth the cost. Other critics worry about issues of identity theft and the dangers of working with dangerous substances. The biggest criticism of e-cycling, however, is that e-cycling exploits third world countries and endangers land, water, and people in areas that have few worker or environmental protections. Most of Americans' e-waste is being sent to developing countries like India and Nigeria, where it is stripped of whatever is valuable—with the rest ending up in landfills, rivers, lakes, and empty fields. Workers handle toxic substances without the proper safety equipment. According to many critics, the United States is just shifting the dangers and costs of e-cycling to more vulnerable workforces.

The debate over e-cycling is one of the topics explored in the following chapter. Other viewpoints in the chapter examine the reprocessing of nuclear waste, the Yucca Mountain nuclear waste facility controversy, and the viability of fly ash landfills.

> "The repository at Yucca Mountain was only made necessary by our failure to understand a fundamental fact about nuclear power: There is no such thing as nuclear waste."

Nuclear Waste Should Be Reprocessed

William Tucker

In the following viewpoint, author William Tucker states that what the American public thinks of as nuclear waste is actually nuclear material that can be easily reprocessed and recycled as fuel or other useful material. Tucker traces the misconception back to the mid-1970s, when there was great fear that foreign powers or terrorists would steal plutonium to build nuclear bombs—spent fuel was then stored and guarded, not reprocessed.

As you read, consider the following questions:

1. How much of a spent fuel rod is made of uranium-238, according to the author?

2. What percentage of the earth's crust is made of uranium-238, according to Tucker?

3. What country does the viewpoint indicate completely reprocesses its nuclear material?

"White House Buries Yucca," read the headlines last week [in March 2009] after Secretary of Energy Steven Chu said the proposed storage of nuclear waste in a Nevada mountain is "no longer an option."

Instead, Mr. Chu told a Senate hearing, the [Barack] Obama administration will cut all but the most rudimentary funding to Yucca and be content to allow spent fuel rods to sit in storage pools and dry casks at reactor sites "while the administration devises a new strategy toward nuclear waste disposal."

Nevada Sen. Harry Reid, a longtime opponent of the repository, was overjoyed. Environmental groups were equally gratified, since they have long seen Yucca Mountain as a choke point for asphyxiating nuclear energy. Greenpeace immediately called for an end to new construction of nuclear power plants, and for all existing reactors to be closed down.

So is this really the death knell for nuclear power? Not at all. The repository at Yucca Mountain was only made necessary by our failure to understand a fundamental fact about nuclear power: There is no such thing as nuclear waste.

No Nuclear Waste?

A nuclear fuel rod is made up of two types of uranium: U-235, the fissionable isotope whose breakdown provides the energy; and U-238, which does not fission and serves basically as packing material. Uranium-235 makes up only 0.7% of the natural ore. In order to reach "reactor grade," it must be "enriched" up to 3%—an extremely difficult industrial process. (To become bomb material, it must be enriched to 90%, another ball game altogether.)

After being loaded in a nuclear reactor, the fuel rods sit for five years before being removed. At this point, about 12

The Global State of Reprocessing

When France built the La Hague facility in 1966, the United States had a fledgling reprocessing program under way, but President [Gerald] Ford froze the program in 1976, concluding that the proliferation risks from reprocessing were too great. The next year, President [Jimmy] Carter announced that the United States would "defer indefinitely" the commercialization of reprocessing and recycling. President [Ronald] Reagan lifted the ban in 1981, but no company chose to pursue reprocessing on a completely private basis.

The United Kingdom, Germany, Russia and India also started programs. Germany closed its facilities in 2005, and the United Kingdom's facilities have run into serious management and financial difficulties. Japan is planning on opening its Rokkasho reprocessing facilities later this year [2009], which will be followed by a MOX [mixed-oxide-fuel] plant in 2015.

Katherine Ling,
"Is the Solution to the U.S. Nuclear Waste Problem in France?,"
New York Times, May 18, 2009.

ounces of U-235 will have been completely transformed into energy. But that's enough to power San Francisco for five years. There are no chemical transformations in the process and no carbon dioxide emissions.

When they emerge, the fuel rods are intensely radioactive—about twice the exposure you would get standing at ground zero at Hiroshima after the bomb went off. But because the amount of material is so small—it would fit comfortably in a tractor-trailer—it can be handled remotely through well-established industrial processes. The spent rods

123

are first submerged in storage pools, where a few yards of water block the radioactivity. After a few years, they can be moved to lead-lined casks about the size of a gazebo, where they can sit for the better part of a century until the next step is decided.

Usable Material

So is this material "waste"? Absolutely not. Ninety-five percent of a spent fuel rod is plain old U-238, the nonfissionable variety that exists in granite tabletops, stone buildings and the coal burned in coal plants to generate electricity. Uranium-238 is 1% of the earth's crust. It could be put right back in the ground where it came from.

Of the remaining 5% of a rod, one-fifth is fissionable U-235—which can be recycled as fuel. Another one-fifth is plutonium, also recyclable as fuel. Much of the remaining three-fifths has important uses as medical and industrial isotopes. Forty percent of all medical diagnostic procedures in this country now involve some form of radioactive isotope, and nuclear medicine is a $4 billion business. Unfortunately, we must import all our tracer material from Canada, because all of our isotopes have been headed for Yucca Mountain.

What remains after all this material has been extracted from spent fuel rods are some isotopes for which no important uses have yet been found, but which can be stored for future retrieval. France, which completely reprocesses its recyclable material, stores all the unused remains—from 30 years of generating 75% of its electricity from nuclear energy—beneath the floor of a single room at La Hague.

The Hoax of Nuclear Waste

The supposed problem of "nuclear waste" is entirely the result of a decision in 1976 by President Gerald Ford to suspend reprocessing, which President Jimmy Carter made permanent in

1977. The fear was that agents of foreign powers or terrorist groups would steal plutonium from American plants to manufacture bombs.

That fear has proved to be misguided. If foreign powers want a bomb, they will build their own reactors or enrichment facilities, as North Korea and Iran have done. The task of extracting plutonium from highly radioactive material and fashioning it into a bomb is far beyond the capacities of any terrorist organization.

So shed no tears for Yucca Mountain. Instead of ending the nuclear revival, it gives us the chance to correct a historical mistake and follow France's lead in developing complete reprocessing for nuclear material.

| "Reprocessing is not a sensible answer to the nuclear waste problem."

Nuclear Waste Should Not Be Reprocessed

Union of Concerned Scientists

The Union of Concerned Scientists is a science-based, nonprofit organization. In the following viewpoint, the group contends that the recent push toward reprocessing spent nuclear fuel has been spurred by false claims by the reprocessing industry. In fact, the group claims, the reprocessing would increase, not decrease, the amount of nuclear waste and exacerbate the problem of nuclear waste disposal in the United States. One of the main problems with the reprocessing systems being proposed, the group argues, is that the storage methods cannot be guaranteed to be safe for future generations.

As you read, consider the following questions:

1. How many spent nuclear fuel rods does the viewpoint state are produced every year in the United States?

2. What claims has AREVA made about reprocessing?

3. What US government agency disputes AREVA's statement?

"Reprocessing and Nuclear Waste: Reprocessing Would Increase Total Volume of Radioactive Waste," Union of Concerned Scientists, July 2009. Reproduced by permission.

Each year in the United States, nuclear power reactors produce about 2,000 tons of spent nuclear fuel rods. This highly radioactive waste, which will remain dangerous for hundreds of thousands of years, is currently stored at the reactor sites where it is generated. According to current law, spent nuclear fuel and other "high-level" radioactive wastes can be disposed of only in a deep geologic repository where they can be isolated from the environment. However, the U.S. government has developed only one site for such a repository, Yucca Mountain in Nevada, which has experienced significant technical difficulties and political opposition. The [Barack] Obama administration has decided to stop development of Yucca Mountain, and reactor owners will likely continue to store spent fuel on-site for several decades. Fortunately, there is no near-term need for a permanent repository, since spent fuel can be stored safely and securely in dry casks for at least 50 years. However, the long-term storage problem must be resolved.

Yucca Mountain's cancellation has led to renewed interest in spent fuel reprocessing, which is a complex chemical process that dissolves spent nuclear fuel in acid and separates its various constituents: uranium, plutonium and highly radioactive isotopes known as "fission products."

Misleading Claims by AREVA

The interest in reprocessing is partly based on false claims by the reprocessing industry that the technology simplifies the nuclear waste disposal problem by reducing the hazard and volume of waste. For instance, AREVA [a French conglomerate that specializes in nuclear power], in which the French government has a 90 percent share, is trying to obtain U.S. government funding to build a reprocessing plant in the United States and claims that reprocessing "reduces the volume of waste by a factor of at least four." This statement is contradicted by recent data from the U.S. Department of En-

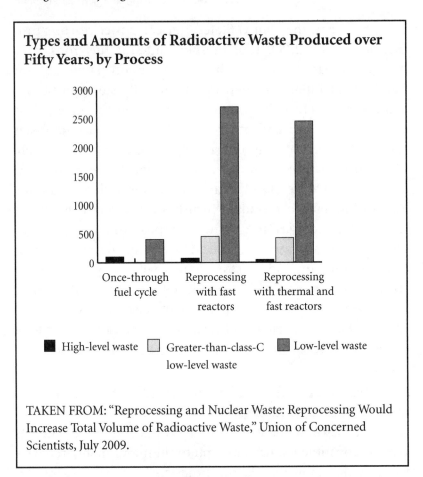

Types and Amounts of Radioactive Waste Produced over Fifty Years, by Process

■ High-level waste ▢ Greater-than-class-C low-level waste ▨ Low-level waste

TAKEN FROM: "Reprocessing and Nuclear Waste: Reprocessing Would Increase Total Volume of Radioactive Waste," Union of Concerned Scientists, July 2009.

ergy (DOE), which show that reprocessing greatly increases the total volume of radioactive waste, compared to direct disposal of spent fuel.

The [data show] the volume of different waste streams generated by three different reactor fuel cycles. In the "once-through" cycle, which reflects the current U.S. strategy, the spent fuel is stored and ultimately disposed of in a geologic repository. In the second fuel cycle, all spent fuel would be reprocessed and the plutonium extracted from reprocessing would be used as new fuel in advanced "fast burner" reactors, which are yet to be developed. The third scenario is similar to the second, except that the recovered plutonium would be used in both fast reactors and current-generation "thermal" reactors. A geologic repository would still be required in scenarios 2 and 3, since reprocessing generates high-level radioactive waste.

In addition to high-level waste, reprocessing generates other types of radioactive waste that require secure disposal. These wastes are more dilute than high-level waste (and hence have greater volume). Although most of the waste falls into the low-level waste category, reprocessing increases the volume by a factor of six to seven relative to the once-through cycle. The United States has three NRC [Nuclear Regulatory Commission]-licensed, commercially operated low-level waste disposal sites that currently accept waste. Reprocessing increases the volume of greater-than-class-C low-level waste by a factor of 160. DOE is responsible for disposing of this waste, which contains long-lived radioactive isotopes and cannot be placed in a regular low-level waste site, but as yet has no policy on how to do so.

Relative to the once-through cycle, reprocessing results in somewhat less high-level waste requiring disposal in a geologic repository (23–24 percent by volume). However, this benefit would be insignificant compared to the additional burden posed by the large volumes of low-level and greater-than-class-C wastes.

The data reflect DOE's assumption that the radioactive isotopes cesium-137 and strontium-90 would also be separated during reprocessing, and stored aboveground in dry casks for 300 years, during which they would decay to very low concentrations. However, the safety of such aboveground storage containers cannot be guaranteed for 300 years because they would not maintain their structural integrity and would need to be replaced. Moreover, proposing a waste "solution" that poses a risk for the next dozen generations is irresponsible.

Additional Reprocessing Waste

The data underestimate the waste produced by reprocessing, because DOE did not provide data on two additional reprocessing waste streams.

First, uranium would be separated during reprocessing and stored as an oxide powder in drums. The volume of the separated uranium would be comparable to that of the initial spent fuel. While in principle this material could be re-enriched for use as reactor fuel, it is contaminated with undesirable uranium and plutonium isotopes, making it far more expensive and inconvenient than using mined uranium. Thus, DOE would likely classify this material as greater-than-class-C low-level waste.

Second, the decontamination and decommissioning of reprocessing and fuel fabrication plants would generate additional waste. DOE asserts that it does not need to account for these wastes because they would be much smaller than those from the reactor fleet. However, this claim is not plausible and DOE should include this waste to provide an accurate comparison of the waste produced in the once-through and reprocessing scenarios.

The Rest of the Story

Finally, a system of fast reactors operating over a period of a century or longer would be needed to consume the plutonium and other actinides that are separated during reprocessing. Each reactor cycle consumes only a small fraction of these elements, so the spent fuel would have to be repeatedly reprocessed and reused over many years. If this system shuts down at some point, the remaining material would end up as waste and need to be disposed of in a repository.

The Bottom Line

Reprocessing of spent nuclear fuel would increase, not decrease, the total volume of nuclear waste. AREVA's claims to the contrary are inaccurate. Reprocessing is not a sensible answer to the nuclear waste problem.

"In shuttering Yucca Mountain, [President Barack] Obama makes it extremely likely that nuclear power in the United States will continue its long, slow, and extremely welcome death."

The Yucca Mountain Nuclear Waste Facility Should Be Closed

Timothy Noah

Timothy Noah is a senior writer for Slate.com. In the following viewpoint, he lauds the Obama administration's decision to close down the Yucca Mountain nuclear waste facility, noting the current practice of storing spent fuel rods is impractical and dangerous. Noah argues that the closing will give officials a chance to reevaluate America's nuclear power and nuclear waste policies to find a better solution in light of new technologies.

As you read, consider the following questions:

1. What was the length of time that the Bush administration was preparing to guarantee the safe storage of spent nuclear fuel rods inside Yucca Mountain, according to Noah?

2. What does Noah state was the first year nuclear waste was going to be stored at Yucca Mountain?

3. According to Noah, how many applications for new nuclear reactors are under consideration by the Nuclear Regulatory Commission?

We've seen a lot of hyperbole lately about the significance of a presidency that's all of six weeks old. I hesitate to add to it. But the following statement happens to be the literal truth.

The ramifications of the 2008 presidential election will be felt for 1 million years.

Long-Term Implications

One million years is a long time. A million years ago, *Homo erectus* was getting ready to invent the hand axe and discover fire. Yet 1 million years is the length of time that the Bush administration was preparing to guarantee (apparently to our successor hominid species) the safe storage of spent nuclear fuel rods inside Nevada's Yucca Mountain, in a waste facility whose approval had been making its way through three branches of government for a comparatively brief 32 years. The goal was to start dumping this high-level nuclear waste inside Yucca Mountain in 2020. Here is how the Bush Department of Energy forecast the year 1,002,020 A.D. in a safety report issued this past June [2008] when it submitted an application for Yucca Mountain's approval to the Nuclear Regulatory Commission:

Imagining the initial quantity of radioactivity emplaced in the repository as 1,500 marbles, natural radioactive decay would leave 270 marbles after 1,000 years and only 90 marbles after 10,000 years. By 100,000 years, there would be only eight marbles left. Finally, after 1 million years, just one marble out of the original 1,500 would remain ... about 99.93 percent of the radioactivity originally placed in the repository would have decayed.

This constituted remarkable long-term planning for an administration that refused to provide 10-year budget projections. It was imposed from without. Originally, Yucca Mountain required "only" a 10,000-year safety guarantee, but in 2004 a federal court insisted on a million-year standard, citing concerns in a 1995 study by the National Academy of Sciences [NAS] that the nuclear waste would take much longer than 10,000 years to reach maximum exposure levels. The NAS had said a reasonably accurate assessment could be made of the site's geology over the next million years. (After that, not so much!) The Environmental Protection Agency duly issued its first-ever million-year regulation, setting a maximum legal limit for release of radioactive materials at 15 millirem per year for the first 10,000 years and 100 millirem for the next 990,000. Nevadans of the 10,021st century would have to figure out themselves what to do about the 0.07 percent remnant left in that last marble.

Closing Down Yucca Mountain

The entire discussion was, of course, outlandishly hubristic. It was made necessary by the outlandishly severe and long-lasting environmental dangers posed by nuclear waste. Six decades after the dawn of the nuclear era, the only plausible answer to the question "What do we do with this stuff?" is "Don't create any more of it." That, in effect, is what President [Barack] Obama is saying in fulfilling his campaign promise to shut down Yucca Mountain. The program, Obama's new budget states, "will be scaled back to those costs necessary to answer

Closing Yucca Mountain

The U.S. Department of Energy moved to terminate Yucca Mountain in March 2010 when it asked the Nuclear Regulatory Commission to withdraw a two-year-old application to build a repository. Calling Yucca Mountain "not a workable option," the Energy Department said the science on nuclear waste storage had evolved since the project was first proposed.

Tennille Tracy,
"New Fight Breaks Out on Nuclear Dump Site,"
Wall Street Journal, *January 31, 2011.*

inquiries from the Nuclear Regulatory Commission while the administration devises a new strategy toward nuclear waste disposal." That's bureaucratese for "Yucca Mountain is dead."

Had John McCain been elected, Yucca Mountain would be headed toward final NRC approval, possibly before the next presidential election (though Senate Majority Leader Harry Reid of Nevada, a longtime opponent, would be trying very hard to prevent that). During the campaign, McCain favored opening Yucca Mountain for business even while telling an interviewer that he would never permit transport of nuclear waste through his home state of Arizona en route to Nevada (with which Arizona shares a border). The Obama campaign made gleeful use of the clip. McCain's worry about the transport of high-level nuclear waste is well-founded; routinely hauling this stuff by truck or rail poses serious risk of a catastrophic accident.

Alternatives to Yucca

The nuclear industry has long argued, correctly, that the current practice of storing spent fuel rods on-site in water-filled vaults and, after those fill up, transferring them to steel-reinforced dry concrete casks is impractical. Though the industry is loath to point out safety concerns, it has repeatedly noted that storage space is running out. In 1977, President Jimmy Carter effectively ended the reprocessing of spent nuclear fuel in civilian plants, and it's doubtful that will be reversed during an era of homeland security. (In truth, the end product of reprocessing, plutonium would be fantastically difficult for terrorists to steal safely, but reprocessing creates environmental headaches of its own.) What should nuclear power plants do? "Our position," says Kevin Kamps, a radioactive-waste expert at the environmental group Beyond Nuclear, "is that we should not be creating this material to begin with." Since 2006, environmental groups have recommended limiting the density of existing water-filled vaults and hardening the dry casks. The Obama administration will likely end up doing something along these lines.

Global warming has caused some policy experts to call for a revival of nuclear power, whose expansion halted after the Three Mile Island accident in 1979. Currently there are 20 applications for new reactors under active consideration at the NRC. As recently as 2007, there were none. Nuclear plants are indeed vastly preferable to coal-fired plants from the standpoint of carbon dioxide emissions. But you can't just take into account the waste that power plants *don't* create. In shuttering Yucca Mountain, Obama makes it extremely likely that nuclear power in the United States will continue its long, slow, and extremely welcome death. For the next couple of decades, anyway. That's as far out as I'm willing to predict anything.

> "A long history of opposition to [a nuclear waste storage facility at Yucca Mountain] makes it very difficult for some Nevada politicians to support the project, despite growing evidence of its technical soundness and general safety."

The Yucca Mountain Nuclear Waste Facility Should Not Be Closed

Jack Spencer

Jack Spencer is a research fellow in nuclear energy in the Thomas A. Roe Institute for Economic Policy Studies at the Heritage Foundation. In the following viewpoint, he contends that Yucca Mountain should not be closed, but reconfigured to be more than just a nuclear waste dump. Reinventing Yucca Mountain as a state-of-the-art hub of America's nuclear industry activities, Spencer indicates, would build on the progress that was made toward an effective national nuclear waste disposal policy under President George W. Bush. Spencer views the Barack Obama administration's decision to end the project as an opportunity to redefine the purpose of the facility in order to revive the nuclear power industry and provide new jobs for people in Nevada.

Jack Spencer, "Yucca Mountain and Nuclear Waste Policy: A New Beginning?," Heritage Foundation, December 16, 2009. Reproduced by permission.

As you read, consider the following questions:

1. What existing statutes did the Obama administration ignore when it closed Yucca Mountain, according to Spencer?

2. When does the viewpoint state that Gregory Jaczko ordered a stop to all Yucca-related activities in the Nuclear Regulatory Commission (NRC)?

3. Why does the author believe that the Safety Evaluation Report is critical and should be immediately released to the public?

Senator Harry Reid's (D-NV) re-election campaign against Sharron Angle [in 2010] provides a historic new opportunity to establish a new Yucca Mountain policy that benefits Nevadans and the U.S. Unfortunately, the omnibus spending bill currently under consideration would de-fund the program. While Reid's staunch opposition to the project has brought it close to the point of termination, the end of Yucca would not benefit Nevada or the nation.

Instead, Reid should use his victory to establish a new path forward. As Angle argued throughout her campaign, science and technology have advanced to the point where Yucca Mountain would not simply be a nuclear waste dump; instead, it could provide the underpinning for a commercial nuclear industrial complex. Such a development would bring jobs to Nevada and help the U.S. solve its used nuclear fuel dilemma.

Wasting Away

Despite growing political and public support for nuclear power, progress toward actually building any new plants has been a struggle. While the blame for this stagnation often goes to inefficient government subsidy programs, the real problem lies in why those subsidies are necessary to begin with. Chief among these structural problems is the nation's incoherent nuclear waste policy.

This was a problem prior to the Obama administration. The federal government was legally obliged, according to the Nuclear Waste Policy Act (NWPA) of 1982, as amended, to begin collecting nuclear waste in 1998. Despite collecting approximately $30 billion (fees plus interest) from electricity ratepayers and spending nearly $10 billion, it has not collected one atom of nuclear waste. The one bright spot was the progress on Yucca Mountain made by President George W. Bush's Department of Energy (DOE).

The Obama administration's anti-Yucca policy destroyed this progress. It ignored existing statute, such as the NWPA and the Yucca Mountain Development Act of 2002, which state clearly that Yucca Mountain shall be the location of the nation's nuclear materials repository. It unilaterally requested the withdrawal of the DOE's permit application for Yucca to the Nuclear Regulatory Commission (NRC). Questions over the legality of this policy are currently under review by the courts.

Meanwhile, in October 2010, former Reid adviser and current NRC Chairman Gregory Jaczko ordered a stop to all Yucca-related NRC activities. He argued that his authority to close out the Yucca program was derived from President Obama's 2011 budget request. The problem is that neither the House nor the Senate passed that proposed budget. Further, the order ignores the fact that the NRC's own Atomic Licensing and Safety Board agreed unanimously that the DOE lacked authority to withdraw the application. The chairman's actions were so unusual and contentious that fellow NRC commissioners were compelled to publicly denounce the decision.

The combination of federal promises to store nuclear waste, the Obama administration's policy, and the NRC actions has resulted in a complete lack of direction on nuclear

"Sciwence Politics," cartoon by John Trever, March 10, 2009. Copyright © 2009 John Trever, *Albuquerque Journal*, www.PoliticalCartoons.com. All rights reserved.

waste management and a dereliction of responsibility on the part of the federal government to uphold its obligations. This creates substantial government-imposed risk on the nuclear industry, which is the primary obstacle to an expansion of U.S. nuclear power.

A New Beginning for Yucca Mountain

Reid can continue to oppose Yucca under the current plan and simultaneously offer a better solution that would put Nevada's interests first. Currently, the DOE controls and manages spent nuclear fuel policy and the Yucca Mountain repository. A new Reid plan should put Nevada in control.

Such a plan could garner support in Nevada. As Angle demonstrated throughout her campaign, Nevadans are at least open to Yucca under different conditions. Thus, Reid should propose a program that places Nevada in control of the future of Yucca Mountain. Under such a program, Nevada could negotiate directly with the nuclear industry to come up with a mutually beneficial arrangement. While Nevada should not be compelled to open the repository, the state could use the prospect of opening it to create a strong negotiating position.

Unfortunately, the Obama administration and the NRC are about to take that option away from Nevada. To preserve this opportunity, Reid should demand that:

- *The NRC finish its review of the DOE's application to permit the Yucca repository.* The NRC's September 2008 docketing of the DOE's application to construct the repository at Yucca Mountain began a three-year, two-track review process. One track will determine the technical merits of the facility. The other track consists of hearings where parties can challenge the Yucca project. Unfortunately, Jaczko ordered NRC staff to discontinue all activities related to Yucca Mountain, effectively terminating the program. Fellow commissioner Kristin Svinicki described this action as "grossly premature."

- *The NRC publicly release all data, including the Safety Evaluation Report.* The technical and scientific conclusions of the Yucca permit application review were scheduled for release in a Safety Evaluation Report (SER) in November 2010. By closing the books on Yucca now, the chairman prevents this critical document—which taxpayers and ratepayers already paid for—from being published. Publication of the SER is critical because it would provide a final determination on the technical feasibility of the Yucca project. Even if Yucca never progresses, there is no reason to deny Americans access to this informative document.

- *The permit to construct Yucca Mountain be transferred to a third party.* If the NRC issues the permit, Reid should seek avenues to make the license available to a third party, such as a private-sector nonprofit or even the state of Nevada. The new permit holder could then negotiate a workable solution that would fully represent the interests of all parties. This process of negotiation was absent from the original decision to name Yucca the waste repository site.

- *The Blue Ribbon Commission on America's Nuclear Future consider Yucca Mountain.* While the text of the presidential memorandum establishing the commission prudently directs commissioners to consider all alternatives without specifically excluding Yucca, the president's actions to terminate the program clearly communicate otherwise. Taking Yucca off the table erodes the credibility of both the commission and the president's ultimate decision and the ability of Nevada to pursue a different Yucca strategy.

- *At least a minimal amount of funding be made available to keep the Yucca project alive.* Instead of starving Yucca of funds, providing funds under the condition that the Yucca program be reformed to better reflect the interests of Nevada would help Nevadans and the broader United States.

Opportunity Lost, Opportunity Gained

A long history of opposition to Yucca makes it very difficult for some Nevada politicians to support the project, despite growing evidence of its technical soundness and general safety. This was unfortunate, as Nevada could have benefited greatly from the economic impact of such a facility.

However, this opportunity lost is opportunity gained. While the repository at Yucca would have generated jobs for Nevada, the reality is that the program was still flawed. Reid now has the opportunity to establish a new path forward on Yucca Mountain. Such reform would not only help to establish a new industry in Nevada; it would help bring nuclear power back to the U.S.

> "While there are good points on both sides of this argument; the big picture is about our country's choices for energy independence."

Fly Ash Landfills Are a Safe Solution to Coal Ash Waste

Brock Hill

Brock Hill is the mayor of Cumberland County, Tennessee. In the following viewpoint, he states that in his position as mayor he initially opposed a proposed fly ash landfill in Cumberland County until he began investigating fly ash landfills in greater detail. Hill maintains that after hours of expert testimony and interviews, he realizes how safe and cost-effective fly ash landfills are, and he feels very comfortable having one in his town. He also argues that fly ash landfills are ecologically beneficial.

As you read, consider the following questions:

1. How does the Environmental Protection Agency classify coal combustion products, as reported by the author?

2. What percentage of fly ash ends up in landfills, according to Hill?

Brock Hill, "Health Facts About Fly Ash on Web," *Crossville Chronicle*, January 14, 2010. Reproduced by permission.

3. According to Hill, how much of the energy produced in the United States comes from coal?

Radiation from atom bombs has been on most people's minds since Hiroshima and the end of World War II. With Hitler and Tojo out of the way, atomic radioactivity became a very real concern and entered popular culture as the new force of evil in our universe. American politicians and crazed third world dictators used it to their manipulative advantage. Newspapers and magazines used it to sell more newspapers and magazines. Science fiction authors and playwrights used it effectively as a plot device. Movie producers used it freely to explain the otherwise unexplainable.

Most anyone over 45 will recall watching old black-and-white science fiction movies. In Crossville, you could see two for the price of one at a double feature at the Palace Theatre. They were also shown for free on late-night TV.

One of the best of this genre was *The Attack of the Crab Monsters*, wherein fallout from an atom bomb causes normal-sized crabs on a Pacific Island to transmogrify into giant talking crabs. These atomic "crab monsters" then prey on a group of scientists and after devouring each, take on their speech patterns, personalities, and intellect. Using their newfound people skills, the crab monsters lure new victims into dark, scary caves and to their demise. Of course, Tennessee is nowhere near the beach, but, as a child, these atomic crabs scared the heck out of me.

What with giant crab monsters and other salesmen of atomic fear impregnating our consciousness from birth and beyond; it's no wonder the word "radioactive" scares us. Most of us know that radiation appears naturally in our universe. It is also in a space heater, microwave oven, and radio waves. Of course, it comes in very deadly forms. Last year [2009], it was even used as poison to kill a KGB [abbreviated name of the State Security Agency of Belarus, formerly Soviet national security agency] agent.

The Truth About Fly Ash

Fly ash is what is left after coal in burned. It has been around ever since man began to burn coal. Some may remember dumping it and spreading it in our gardens and yards. It is also beneficially reused in cement and gypsum board in buildings. It is also used to build roads. Fly ash, according to the scientists at the United States Environmental Protection Agency [EPA], contains some trace elements of chemicals that appear naturally in our universe and are radioactive. The Environmental Protection Agency classifies fly ash and other coal combustion products as "diffuse," or naturally occurring radioactive materials, which is EPA's most benign radioactive classification. Studies have shown that the level of radioactivity in fly ash and other coal-combustion products is about the same as the level found in surface rocks and common everyday soil. This and other health information regarding coal combustion products like fly ash is available on the EPA Web site. . . .

However, fly ash can be a health risk if inhaled. That is why it is buried. In fact, fly ash, an inorganic material, is buried in landfills all over America. Since only about 40 percent of fly ash is currently beneficially reused, the remaining 60 percent must go somewhere; so there are hundreds of fly ash landfills in America. The Association of State and Territorial Solid Waste Management Officials recently polled all fifty states to determine what they do with fly ash and other coal combustion products. Some states, like Tennessee, require a thick plastic lining and environmental standards before you can dispose the ash in a landfill. Some states don't require anything. Thirty-six states report no problems with the fly ash inside their borders. Eight states don't have coal combustion products. The others don't report anything. That report is available on the Web. . . .

Reject Fearmongering

Here in Cumberland County, there are many in our community spreading fly ash atomic fears. Of course, science fiction makes for a better story than science truth. Science truth is routine and boring. Science fiction engages its public and won't let go; maybe like being grabbed by a giant crab monster.

Some folks would have us believe that we are being lured to our demise by atomic fly ash salesmen. However, the science truth tells us it is the atomic fear salesman who wants to take over our speech patterns, our personalities, and, especially, our intellect.

When I first heard of the proposed fly ash landfill in Cumberland County, my initial reaction was to oppose the effort. However, I began extensive research to determine the facts. I spoke to government officials who regulate coal mines, water quality, and landfills. I spoke to scientists and engineers outside of government. I spoke to other communities where fly ash is currently being landfilled. I invited representatives from the [Tennessee] Department of Environment and Conservation to address the commission and general public in a meeting at the courthouse. We were assured by them that fly ash, once buried in a landfill, is safe and harmless. Of course, Cumberland County does not permit mine closures or issue landfill permits. Our involvement was in regard to the land-use provisions associated with the potential placement of the landfill on rural and isolated Smith Mountain. The final decision is up to state and federal regulators. If they determine that this project is sound from a scientific and legal perspective, who are we to say it is not? Likewise, if it is not safe, I hope it is denied. No one, especially me, would want to invite an environmental hazard into Cumberland County.

A Favorable Vote

I have no idea what processes the members of the Cumberland County Commission engaged in to come to their conclusions. Apparently they chose to ignore the science of the atomic fear salesmen and instead support the economic benefits of landfill host fee funds that will total millions of dollars and can be invested in education, fire safety, county roads, and economic and community development. There was also talk of potential jobs for local truck drivers. The vote was 11 to 5. While residents along the Smith Mountain Road were disappointed over the vote, commissioners were aware that many knew there was a coal mine at the top of their rural mountain road when they purchased their non-zoned property. The lawsuit brought against Cumberland County by the Smith Mountain Road residents regarding this issue was dismissed by the Chancellor this month [January 2010].

Hysteria on both sides of this issue notwithstanding, this drama contains only a bit part for fly ash. The real star is coal and the plot is more contrived than that of the crab monsters.

Over half of the energy produced in America comes from the burning of coal. As we all know, the mining of coal has always been a messy and dangerous business. In spite of safety precautions, coal mine disasters in America have claimed many lives. The environmental aftermath of coal mines ranges from open mountaintop strip mines to collapsing mine tunnels. The Smith Mountain fly ash landfill project is intended to lawfully close the ugly scarred landscape at an open mine that currently leaks life-smothering manganese and zinc into our streams and groundwater. Unlike fly ash fears of sick fish downstream from the Kingston spill, coal mine runoff kills all aquatic life. The critters don't get sick; they get sick and die. Add to this the fear of global warming alleged to be caused by carbon releases into the atmosphere, much of that attributed to the burning of fossil fuels like coal, and we have a real issue of concern.

The Context of the Fly Ash Landfill Debate

However, coal is cheap. There is plenty of coal in America and the government regulations and our politicians that make those regulations keep it cheap. New technologies, such as wind and solar energy, are having a tough time in the marketplace of ideas due to the comparative advantage of coal due to its low cost. Frustrated investors in those new technologies and their friends in the environmental community want to eliminate that advantage by making coal cost more or by eliminating the burning of coal entirely.

One way to do that is to get fly ash classified as a hazardous material, a legal term, by the Environmental Protection Agency. While there are currently many places to landfill fly ash, there are very few hazardous material storage sites and those are very remote. Make it expensive to store fly ash and the price goes up for burning coal; then the cost advantage is reduced.

As you know, the current global warming legislation being debated in Washington will create a carbon cap-and-trade system. Under that system, many energy producers that burn coal will be forced to purchase carbon credits from carbon-friendly industries. That will also add to the cost of burning coal. All of this will, of course, be passed along to the consumer, but it will pave the way for new energy technologies.

I like the concept of cleaner energy technologies and a cleaner environment. Don't we all?

However, putting these issues in the proper context helps to better understand them. While there are good points on both sides of this argument, the big picture is about our country's choices for energy independence. That will be a drama that we all play a role in; one that our future generations will enjoy hearing about and, hopefully, enjoy the benefits of our efforts.

In the meantime, we need to keep our discussions honest so we can achieve real solutions that will sustain our ecosystems, our economy, and our unique American way of life.

> *"Because of lax government oversight and bureaucratic loopholes, coal ash landfill operators . . . have polluted groundwater at their plants for years without a single fine."*

Fly Ash Landfills and Ponds Create Health Hazards

Tony Bartelme

Tony Bartelme is a reporter for the Post and Courier *in Charleston, South Carolina. In the following viewpoint, he maintains that recent contamination cases across the country, as well as a growing body of research, confirm there is widespread pollution by toxic coal ash. Bartelme argues that while coal industry officials downplay the danger, it has become increasingly clear that fly ash landfills are not a safe or effective way to dispose of coal ash. Despite the danger presented by coal ash disposal, Bartelme insists, government and the coal industry have ignored warnings and have allowed the contamination of water supplies and damage to wildlife.*

Tony Bartelme, "Coal's Time Bomb," *Post and Courier*, October 26, 2008. Reproduced by permission.

As you read, consider the following questions:

1. How many pounds of coal ash does Bartelme state are dumped in landfills and holding ponds every year?

2. As stated by the author, according to an EPA analysis in 2005, how many cases were there in which ash waste tainted groundwater and lakes?

3. In 2006, how much coal ash was generated by coal plants, according to the viewpoint?

Every year, South Carolina's power plants burn enough coal to fill 10 large football stadiums, leaving behind a stadium-size pile of toxic ash.

Every year, our power companies dump roughly 2.3 billion pounds of this tainted ash in landfills and holding ponds, many precariously close to rivers and neighborhoods.

And every year, some of these landfills and ponds leak. Scattered across South Carolina, these vast pits and ponds of coal ash are polluting groundwater and waterways with arsenic, selenium and other chemicals that can cause health problems in wildlife and people, a *Post and Courier* watchdog investigation found.

Water under some landfills has concentrations of arsenic many times the federal limit, documents obtained under the S.C. Freedom of Information Act show.

Consider:

- Near Moncks Corner, in the quiet Whitesville community, arsenic-laced water from a coal ash landfill is leaking into a nearby pond.

- Farther north, near Congaree National Park, arsenic 200 to 400 times the federal drinking water limit has been found in groundwater at SCE&G's plant on the banks of the Wateree River.

- On the Savannah River, SCE&G's Urquhart plant has groundwater tainted with arsenic eight times above the federal standard.

- Closer to Charleston, near Canadys, a breach in an earthen wall at two ash ponds allowed arsenic and nickel to pollute groundwater next to the Edisto River.

- Arsenic levels at Santee Cooper's Grainger coal plant in Conway measured more than 900 parts per billion, 90 times higher than the federal drinking water limit. Significant contamination also has been found in coal ash ponds at the Savannah River site.

Because of lax government oversight and bureaucratic loopholes, coal ash landfill operators here have polluted groundwater at their plants for years without a single fine.

So far, contamination is limited to the landfill operators' properties and the groundwater below, according to engineers with utilities and the state Department of Health and Environmental Control. They say that they're unaware of anyone being sickened by coal waste. Officials with SCE&G and Santee Cooper say their ash disposal operations are in full compliance with state and federal laws.

Still, while coal and other industry interests downplay the dangers of coal ash, it's increasingly clear that many ash ponds and landfills have caused serious pollution problems here and across the nation.

An analysis last year by the U.S. Environmental Protection Agency found 67 cases in 26 states where ash waste tainted groundwater and lakes.

A different EPA study found that people who live next to certain types of coal ash landfills and ponds have a higher risk of getting cancer.

Meanwhile, residents in other states are filing lawsuits alleging that ash basins polluted their drinking wells. In Maryland, state regulators recently fined a utility $1 million over a leaking coal ash pit.

The debate over coal ash has been simmering for years, eclipsed by more heated exchanges about mountaintop removal in Appalachia and coal's role in global warming. That could change.

Earlier this year, South Carolina health officials tightened ash disposal rules—after years of allowing landfill operators to treat ash as if it were no more dangerous than a pile of construction debris.

Meanwhile, Santee Cooper wants to build a new ash landfill and pond next to its proposed Pee Dee coal plant, and SCE&G is building a new landfill near Congaree National Park. Citizens groups and nearby residents are fighting both projects.

All this is happening at a time when the ash itself is likely to grow more contaminated. To comply with clean-air laws, utilities are shelling out hundreds of millions of dollars to better scrub pollutants from their smokestacks. But this scrubbing process can produce ash with higher levels of arsenic, mercury and other poisons.

Put another way, as coal-burning utilities try to clean the air, they may create new environmental challenges on the ground and in the water.

Dangerous and Useful

Coal combustion waste is usually made of fly ash, bottom ash and sludge from air scrubbers.

Bottom ash looks like chunks of black volcanic rock and comes from the bottom of a furnace. Fly ash is lighter and once flew out of chimneys of coal-fired power plants. Fly ash contributed to "killer smogs," such as the one in 1948 in Donora, Pa., that sickened 5,910 of the town's 14,000, and an even deadlier blanket of soot that smothered London in 1952 and killed 4,000 people.

Pollution laws in the United States now require coal-burning utilities to capture nearly all fly ash before it gets into

Dangers of Fly Ash Landfills

"Research has made it clear that coal ash is becoming increasingly toxic. In fact the cancer risk of people living near some coal ash sites is a staggering 1 in 50," said Mary Anne Hitt, deputy director of the Sierra Club's Beyond Coal Campaign.

"EPA Data Reveal Far Reach of Toxic Coal Ash Threats,"
Earth Justice, August 31, 2009.

the air. Not only has this helped clear our skies, it also forced utilities to find more creative ways to send less of the stuff to landfills.

Fortunately, it turns out that coal ash is surprisingly useful.

Put fly ash under a microscope, and you'll see tiny glasslike spheres. When you put these spheres in concrete, they fill voids and create a ball-bearing effect that makes the concrete more durable. The Romans knew this and used volcanic ash in the Coliseum and Pantheon.

More recently, the equivalent of 330 trainloads of fly ash went into concrete for the new Cooper River bridge's diamond towers, which required a concrete of extra-high density. Bottom ash, meanwhile, can be used to make lighter concrete blocks, and scrubber sludge can be turned into wallboard. Some ash can even be incorporated into bowling balls. Santee Cooper, notably, has managed to create programs to reuse more than 85 percent of its ash.

Still, the nation's coal plants crank so much ash—125 million tons in 2006, according to the American Coal Ash Association—that these boilers generate plenty of ash to spare. In

2006, about 70 million tons went into landfills, ash ponds and abandoned mines, sometimes causing environmental headaches.

When ash comes into contact with water, contaminants including arsenic, lead, mercury, selenium and others can migrate into groundwater, lakes and streams. Arsenic is usually the biggest concern. Studies have linked prolonged exposure to arsenic with cancer, digestive problems and other health problems. But scientists also are concerned about selenium and mercury, which also can be dangerous to people and wildlife in small doses.

Last year, the Environmental Protection Agency released a study identifying 67 cases of coal ash waste contamination, including 24 "proven cases" of environmental damage, including two ash ponds in South Carolina—one at the Savannah River site and another next to the SCE&G coal plant near Canadys. Also last year, the EPA released a draft of another study of 181 coal ash sites nationwide that found unlined ash ponds posed a cancer risk hundreds of times more than what the EPA deems acceptable. Scientists with Earthjustice, a group critical of ash basins, said unlined ash pits posed the same kind of danger as smoking a pack of cigarettes a day.

As far back as 2000, the EPA concluded that ash wastes "could pose risks to human health ... and there is sufficient evidence that adequate controls may not be in place." Despite these studies and conclusions, the agency never classified coal ash as a hazardous waste. That enabled coal-burning operations to dump ash in relatively primitive landfills and ponds.

In South Carolina, for instance, utilities and other coal-burning industries, such as MeadWestvaco, only had to have a 2-foot separation between the ash and groundwater. Some landfill operators simply lined the bottoms with compacted dirt.

Mixing Zone Pass

Despite long-standing contamination problems at several South Carolina ash sites, DHEC hasn't issued any fines, a review of agency files and interviews with state environmental officials show.

This is the case even though the utility officials and DHEC have acknowledged in at least one case that pollution laws were violated. Instead, through a little-known law, DHEC grants landfill operators permission to create "mixing zones," a government pass to mix polluted groundwater with clean water.

According to DHEC regulations, landfill operators can create a mixing zone if they try to minimize the contamination in some fashion, and as long as the pollutants aren't dangerous or prone to move much.

How has this mixing zone strategy worked?

SCE&G's Canadys plant provides one answer.

Arsenic and the Edisto

In 1974, SCE&G started dumping ash into a holding pond next to its plant along the Edisto River, and since 1982, scientists have found arsenic and nickel in groundwater, which eventually spread beyond SCE&G's land, according to an EPA report.

To solve the problem, SCE&G "was allowed to buy neighboring property under state policy at the time," the EPA report said.

SCE&G asked DHEC for permission to create a mixing zone below the pond, and DHEC agreed. The power company then built a second ash pond, but arsenic from this new pond also made it into groundwater.

So SCE&G sought DHEC's approval to expand the original mixing zone to cover the new polluting pond, and DHEC once again gave a thumbs up, documents show.

Now, tests show arsenic and selenium in groundwater at the very edge of this larger mixing zone. Some areas are just a short walk from the Edisto and have arsenic levels four times the federal drinking water limit.

Neither DHEC, nor SCE&G, have calculated how much arsenic or selenium may have spread beyond the mixing zone and reached the Edisto River, if any. They also say the ash pond doesn't pose a threat to the public or wildlife.

Younan of SCE&G explained that the arsenic leached into groundwater after a wall at the new ash pond failed. He said the utility spent about $11 million to fix the problem, and did so voluntarily. "I'm not going to sit here and say we didn't have problems at Canadys," he said. "But we identified the problem and jumped right on it, and we had no problem spending $11 million to fix it."

He said this expensive fix should cause arsenic levels outside the mixing zone to decline.

Still, the EPA last year classified the site as one of 24 "proven cases" nationwide of damage to the environment, a classification with which Younan strongly disagrees. "We know we have a problem, and we fixed the problem," he said.

'Fallen Down'

Some critics of ash waste dumps say state and federal agencies have long turned a blind eye to evidence that coal ash waste is a serious pollution issue. "They've fallen down on the job about this waste in a big way," said Jeff Stant, an activist with the Environmental Integrity Project who has studied coal ash issues for more than a decade.

Stant estimates that more than 60 million tons of coal ash is dumped every year without meeting any basic safeguards. He said heavy lobbying by coal and utility interests successfully slowed effective state and federal regulators. "The problem is that they want to keep coal cheap," he said, "but they're doing it on the backs of people and the environment."

The disposal of coal ash will only get more difficult, he added. As utilities install more scrubbers, coal ash will have even higher levels of arsenic, chromium and mercury. These scrubbers also generate higher overall volumes of ash.

Because of this, DHEC in May tightened regulations for ash disposal. New landfills will need better liners and systems to collect water seeping from ash pits. Other states are taking similar measures.

But what about the old landfills?

During the past several years, power companies and other coal ash handlers nationwide have been hit with a number of lawsuits and fines.

In the town of Pines, Indiana, utilities dumped more than a million tons of coal ash in a local landfill and used the material as road fill. Now, after coal ash chemicals were found in drinking wells, Pines is on the EPA's Superfund roster of the nation's most troublesome toxic waste sites.

Earlier this year in Montana, power companies paid $25 million to settle lawsuits by plant workers and residents who alleged that utilities knew they were contaminating water supplies for years before they notified residents.

And, last year, Maryland regulators fined a power company and its contractor $1 million after coal ash buried in an unlined gravel pit poisoned nearby drinking wells.

For years, coal-burning companies, along with federal and state regulators, viewed ash as if it was no more dangerous than dirt. But contamination cases here and across the country, along with a growing body of evidence about the effects of ash on wildlife, raise new questions about how this little-known by-product is handled—and how it will be dealt with in the future.

"*The potential danger of e-waste has been known for years, but there is a growing concern over its proliferation and the lack of transparency about its final resting place.*"

Recycling E-Waste Is Environmentally Beneficial

Rex Springston

Rex Springston is a writer for the Richmond Times-Dispatch. *In the following viewpoint, he observes that many states have banned the disposal of e-waste in landfills due to health and safety concerns. Springston argues that while the growing trend to recycle e-waste has the best intentions, it also raises questions about where the recycling is done and what health precautions are taken for workers overseas.*

As you read, consider the following questions:

1. As reported by the author, how many tons of electronics were discarded in the United States in 2007, according to the Environmental Protection Agency (EPA)?

2. How many tons of e-waste were discarded in 1997, according to Springston?

Rex Springston, "Most Aspects of E-Waste Not Regulated in US, VA," *Richmond Times-Dispatch*, September 19, 2010. Reproduced by permission.

3. As reported by the author, what percentage of e-waste in 2007 ended up in landfills?

Virginians are creating piles of potentially dangerous waste.

The problem is old electronics, or e-waste—computers, cell phones and other gadgets that people toss because they've found something newer and shinier.

"It's not factory waste but post-consumer waste that's coming out of your hands, my hands or anybody's hands," said Jim Puckett, director of the Basel Action Network, a Seattle-based environmental group.

The old electronics are laced with pollutants, such as lead and cadmium, that have been linked to cancer, nervous-system damage and other problems.

No one is sure how much e-waste Virginians produce. No one tracks it closely, in Virginia or nationally. But everyone agrees it's a lot.

The Environmental Protection Agency [EPA] says the U.S. discarded about 2.25 million tons of electronics in 2007, the most recent year for which even a rough estimate is available.

That's about 14 ½ pounds—roughly the weight of a couple of laptops—for every U.S. resident. It's also nearly a threefold increase from the estimated 850,000 tons in 1997, according to the EPA.

"There's so much of it, and it's being generated at an increasing rate in the U.S. and worldwide," said Dan Gallo, an environmental protection specialist for the EPA.

And no one knows precisely where it all goes. Most of it ends up in landfills that are safe now, regulators say, but which critics say will leak someday.

A portion of the waste—the amount is in dispute—gets exported to such places as China and Africa, where workers in unsafe conditions extract valuable copper and other materials using open fires and acid.

Most aspects of e-waste are unregulated, federally and in Virginia.

"We're not deeply involved in how computers are managed in Virginia, other than encouraging that they be recycled or donated so they can have continued life," said Steve Coe, recycling specialist with the state Department of Environmental Quality [DEQ].

The state and federal governments oversee the disposal of cathode-ray tubes, or CRTs—the big, glassy parts in old computer monitors and TVs—which can contain up to 8 pounds of lead, a toxic metal.

But while some states ban residents from dumping CRTs and other electronics in landfills, Virginia does not.

Among Virginia's neighbors, North Carolina and West Virginia will start banning the dumping of computer equipment and TVs next year [2011]. Maryland has no ban or plans for one.

Virginia allows individuals to dump old electronics with their household garbage, which ends up in a landfill.

Virginia localities can ban people from tossing lead-laden CRTs in the trash, but few localities—and none in the Richmond area—do that.

Of the electronics discarded in 2007, more than 80 percent went into landfills, the EPA says. Everyone agrees that's a waste of landfill space and valuable materials that can be recycled. The question is whether that dumping endangers the public.

The EPA says no, because modern landfills are equipped with plastic underground liners and systems designed to limit pollution.

"If properly managed, the disposal of electronics in landfills can be safe," Gallo said.

Others fear that even the most modern liners will leak someday, allowing e-waste-tainted "garbage juice" to pollute underground water, which can feed wells and streams.

States That Have Passed E-Waste Laws

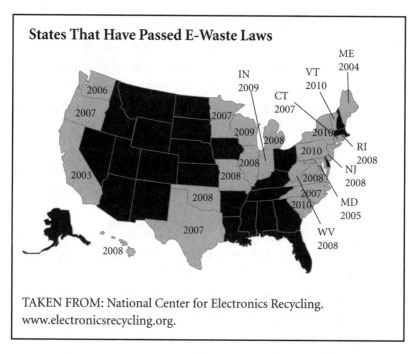

TAKEN FROM: National Center for Electronics Recycling. www.electronicsrecycling.org.

"The heavy metals are there for the long, long term, and I don't think the liners are there for the long, long term," said Roger Diedrich, who deals with waste issues for the Virginia chapter of the Sierra Club. Acidic liquids in landfills can dissolve hazardous metals in e-waste such as lead and copper, said John T. Novak, a Virginia Tech professor of civil and environmental engineering.

If the landfill leaks, those metals can contaminate groundwater, but operators of properly built landfills should prevent that by pumping out and treating the liquids, among other measures, Novak said.

Landfills contain lots of nasty things, including treated wood containing copper and arsenic. You can debate the wisdom of building big landfills, but there is nothing really unique about the threat of the e-waste in them, Novak said.

"A landfill is almost like a biological experiment," said Scott Mouw, North Carolina's recycling director.

"To me, it's common sense" to recycle or reuse electronics, he said, and not put them where they might cause problems.

While most of the high-tech castoffs go into landfills, the rest are either repaired and put back into use, or recycled.

Much of the recycled waste is ultimately broken down into parts such as plastic and metals that can be used to make such products as parking-lot curbs and lead-acid batteries.

Although it sounds wonderful to recycle, critics say a lot of e-waste that is diverted toward recycling gets shipped to developing countries.

"Eighty percent of what you hand over to a recycler in this country is going to end up offshore," said Puckett, the Seattle environmentalist.

The exports can be legal, particularly if they don't involve cathode-ray tubes. But, critics say, some exports endanger overseas workers and mislead Americans who in good faith take their old computers and other items to recycling sites— sometimes paying for the privilege.

The EPA's Gallo said he does not know what portion of the exports is handled improperly, but, "We think it's not as large as what's being portrayed" in the media.

The Government Accountability Office said in a scathing 2008 report that the EPA did little to stop recyclers from sending e-waste overseas. Used electronics other than CRTs flow "virtually unrestricted" to developing countries, the report said.

The EPA is planning a study to better determine the fate of exported electronics, Gallo said.

Robert Houghton, president of Redemtech, an Ohio-based company that repairs and recycles old electronics, said, "I think it's absolutely truthful to say that there are no completely reliable statistics" on where e-waste goes.

Some say Congress will eventually have to stop the improper handling of e-waste.

"We stopped companies from throwing stuff in rivers a long time ago," Houghton said. "This really isn't very different."

The state DEQ's Coe said he believes recycling companies in Virginia are operating properly—partly because they are truly "getting green" and partly because they fear getting bad publicity.

"There's a business risk if they don't do the right thing," Coe said.

Virginia's e-waste in 2009 included 20,370 computers and other electronics owned by state agencies, state officials said. AERC Recycling Solutions, a Pennsylvania-based company, dealt with the electronics at a cost of $217,587. AERC's services included recycling computer parts and erasing data from computer hard drives. AERC runs two warehouse-like plants near Ashland.

In addition, Computer Recycling of Virginia, a nonprofit near Tappahannock, recycled and refurbished since 2006 about 47,000 formerly state-owned computers that were replaced by Northrop Grumman under that company's contract to provide technology services to the state. The payment to Computer Recycling totaled $230,515, Northrop Grumman said.

The potential danger of e-waste has been known for years, but there is a growing concern over its proliferation and the lack of transparency about its ultimate resting place.

"I don't know [where Virginia's e-waste goes] and I don't exactly know how to find out," said Sierra's Diedrich.

Could part of the issue be semantic?

Using the term "e-waste" for valuable used electronics adds to the problem, said Eric Harris, associate counsel for the Institute of Scrap Recycling Industries, a trade group.

"If we keep on calling it a waste," Harris said, "we're encouraging the type of behavior that is associated with waste."

Things would be better, Harris said, if we called the stuff "scrap."

"We're simply exporting a huge environmental problem."

Recycling E-Waste Endangers Third World Countries

ABC News

ABCNews.com is the website for ABC News. In the following viewpoint, edited from the original, the writer suggests Americans should be aware that when they recycle their e-waste it more often than not goes to a third world country that has no worker protection or safety regulation. The writer reports that most e-waste ends up in landfills overseas—or even worse, polluting rivers and air. The writer also contends that privacy and criminal issues can arise when electronics containing personal information are disposed of without proper oversight, and maintains that European countries' practice of requiring electronics manufacturers to recycle discarded products is far superior to the United States' lack of regulation.

As you read, consider the following questions:

1. How much did Americans spend on consumer electronics in 2005, according to the viewpoint?

"Is America Exporting a Huge Environmental Problem?," ABCNews.com, January 6, 2006. Article edited from original. Reproduced by permission.

2. What is the percentage of scrap electronics that the author states ends up in third world countries?

3. Why do experts believe that Europe is ahead of the United States when it comes to recycling e-waste, according to the author?

Americans bought an estimated $125 billion worth of consumer electronics—computers, monitors, cell phones, televisions—this past year [2005]. With hundreds of millions of them becoming obsolete every year in this country, what happens to all the stuff we don't want anymore?

Some of us just hang on to it, or pass it on as hand-me-downs to friends or family. And some of us donate our old tech gadgets and computers to charity.

But the hard truth is that your old clunker of a computer may be more of a burden than a blessing to many charities.

"I've tried to give the equipment to the Salvation Army—they don't take it anymore," one man told *20/20*.

The reality is much of the stuff ends up in the garbage.

E-Waste Is Hazardous Waste

But there's a dirty little secret piling up with those electronics thrown into the garbage. This "e-waste" is tainted with hazardous contaminants.

The average computer monitor contains more than five pounds of lead. Computers can also contain mercury and cadmium. When you multiply that by the millions of outdated computers and monitors, you've got lots of toxins that you don't want to put back into the earth.

It's environmentally unsafe for individuals to just throw out computers and monitors, but federal law prohibits businesses from doing it.

Businesses usually pay electronic recyclers to haul away the old equipment and pull it apart, and if it's done right, pretty much everything can be reused.

Unfortunately, it's not always done right. That's dirty little secret No. 2: Some recyclers may not be recycling everything. Actually, some experts say *most* recyclers aren't recycling everything.

"Eighty percent of all the scrap electronics in the United States end up offshore and usually in third world countries," said Bob Glavin of Chicago, who runs one of the biggest recycling plants in the country.

"I honestly believe there's a secret brotherhood that ships this stuff over there late at night when no one's watching, because none of our competitors do it, but it's all over there," he said.

Waste Dumped Abroad Is Rarely Recyclable or Reusable

Glavin and his son used to export some of their scrap to China, until they went there and saw for themselves what happened to it.

"There was no environmental regulations. There's no safety regulations. There's no data security, because it's not being recycled over there. It's being dumped over there," he said.

"We don't send our trash to China. Why should we send the electronic trash to China?" his son Jim added.

Jim Puckett, coordinator of a group called Basel Action Network, which monitors exports of hazardous waste, also saw what was happening in China firsthand. Three years ago he documented it in a video called *Exporting Harm*.

"What we witnessed was these former farmers cooking circuit boards over little wok-type operations over little coal fires and melting the chips so they could pull them off. These chips would then go to acid strippers using very dangerous acids, dumping all the waste from the process into the river, and that acid process was to extract the tiny bit of gold that was in those chips. It was quite a cyber-age nightmare," he said.

Much of this stuff came from the United States, yet U.S. authorities did nothing. Frustrated, Puckett's group released a second report this past year, this time from Nigeria, where they found the same thing.

"Everywhere there's space—empty lots, swampy areas— they'll throw the cathode-ray tubes, the computer carcasses, the plastic housings and routinely set them ablaze," Puckett said.

Puckett says his group saw dusty warehouses piled high with computers and components exported from the United States and Europe, supposedly bought for Nigerians to fix and use.

According to Puckett, however, "About 75 percent of what they were receiving was not repairable, not usable and was simply dumped and burned in the landfills of Africa."

Exporting Our Problems

That's what's happening to many of the old computers we get rid of. They're sent overseas. We're simply exporting a huge environmental problem.

"The recyclers that are shipping over there certainly know what's going on, and it's good business," said Lauren Roman, an electronics recycler and an expert on the hazardous chemicals found in household electronics.

Still, some recycling brokers *20/20* talked to insisted that sending the machines abroad helped get computers into the hands of societies that need them.

Roman disagrees with that. She said lots of companies should call themselves waste exporters instead of recyclers. And she showed *20/20* just how easy it is to pass yourself off as a responsible recycler.

You can simply print out a certificate declaring yourself an Environmental Protection Agency–certified recycler.

It's that simple, according to Roman, "because there's no such thing, but you can claim it because most of the recyclers out there are."

Personal Data Often Remains on Discarded Computers

And there's one more thing you should worry about when you throw out your old computer. Call it dirty little secret No. 3. And this one affects you very personally.

Everything that's been on your computer's hard drive— unless you know how to wipe it clean—is still there. And it will be there if you donate it to charity, or give it to a friend, or throw it out or recycle it.

When Puckett's group was in Nigeria, they bought hard drives that they discovered had a wealth of private information on them.

"One of these hard drives had documents from the Wisconsin Department of Health Services, another from the World Bank. So even if you are not concerned about the environment, you should be concerned about your very, very private data," he said.

But there are some solutions to the mounting e-waste problem. Let's start with hard drives. One good way to trash your hard drive is literally to trash your hard drive. Smash it by taking a hammer to it.

There are also less barbaric ways, especially if you want someone else to be able to use it. There are programs you can buy or download that will truly get rid of everything.

The growing recycling problem is a bit more complicated. Roman and other advocates say we should do with computers and television monitors and fax machines what we do with soda pop bottles or cans: Pay a fee up front that is returnable to you when you get rid of your electronics properly.

Roman says Europe is far ahead of the United States in this regard. Indeed, in Europe it is the manufacturers who are responsible for taking back and properly recycling old computers.

Here's the bottom line: Now that you know you can't—or at least you shouldn't—ignore this problem, don't throw out your computers. Look into participating in—or starting—a community-based electronics recycling drive.

Periodical and Internet Sources Bibliography

The following articles have been selected to supplement the diverse views presented in this chapter.

Mark Clayton	"The Nuclear Waste Problem: Where to Put It?," *Christian Science Monitor*, March 22, 2010.
William H. Miller	"Stop Letting Nuclear Fund Go to Waste," *Columbia Daily Tribune*, October 31, 2010.
Allyn Milojevich	"Closing Yucca Mountain a Waste," Tennessee Center for Policy Research, July 3, 2010. www.tennesseepolicy.org.
National Public Radio	"After Dump, What Happens to Electronic Waste?," December 21, 2010. www.npr.org.
Oladele A. Ogunseitan	"The Wild West of Electronic Waste," Project Syndicate, January 6, 2010. www.project-syndicate.org.
Amanda Peterka	"Urban Mining," *E Magazine*, November 23, 2008.
William B. Reed	"A Lot of Money Has Been Wasted on Nuclear Waste," *Birmingham News*, December 26, 2010.
Kate Riley	"Obama Administration Should Not Close Yucca Mountain Unilaterally," *Seattle Times*, February 25, 2010.
Jack Spencer and Nicolas Loris	"Nuclear Waste: Do Not Rule Out Yucca Mountain Just Yet, Says House of Representatives," Heritage Foundation, July 20, 2009.
Jack Spencer and Garrett Murch	"Road to Clean Air Runs Through Yucca Mountain," Heritage Foundation, June 9, 2008.
Gary Wolfram	"Nuclear 'Waste' Should Be Recycled, Not Buried," *Grand Rapids Press*, May 15, 2010.

OPPOSING
VIEWPOINTS®
SERIES

CHAPTER 4

What Strategies Will Help Reduce Waste and Save Money?

Chapter Preface

The health care industry generates a lot of garbage. Although no organization or government agency keeps precise records on how much waste hospitals, doctors' offices, clinics, and other health care facilities produce each year, some observers estimate several billion tons of waste are produced annually. That means not only used gauze and bandages, but also recyclable plastic equipment such as containers, syringes, and surgical instruments. Shockingly, much of that equipment in landfills has never even been used; the unused devices come from sterilized surgical kits that are opened in the operating room. While some equipment is used, the other things in the kit are thrown out because they are no longer sterile.

As the industry shifted toward disposable plastic products in the 1980s, it also shifted to creating more and more plastic waste sitting in landfills all over the country. Much of this could be recycled for much less money than it costs to buy new equipment for every procedure. Many hospitals and health care organizations, concerned about rising costs and looking for ways to cut budgets, began to consider the cost of medical equipment. Reprocessing as much of that equipment safely and inexpensively became a practical strategy in American health care.

There are different ways health care institutions can approach the problem of medical waste. One strategy is to concentrate on reducing waste during procedures through a thorough revision of practices, products, and strategies. Less equipment used on the front end means less waste on the back end. Another way to reduce waste is to recover and recycle used equipment. Even plastic devices used a single time can be safely disinfected for further uses. Some initiatives focus on salvaging unused equipment that ends up in the trash and donating it to areas in need, such as hospitals in developing countries or the sites of natural disasters. Another recent and effective strategy is to streamline sterile kits to include only devices that are frequently used in medical procedures.

The main concern about the growing movement to reprocess medical equipment is safety. Throughout history, reusing medical devices was common practice. Metal, glass, or rubber equipment was disinfected and sterilized, and then used again. With the spread of the human immunodeficiency virus (HIV) in the 1980s, however, institutions began to utilize single-use plastic devices, especially syringes, to ensure that equipment was sterile and to quell fears that the medical equipment might facilitate the spread of HIV. Recent studies have addressed health and safety concerns about reprocessing equipment. In 2008 a report by the Government Accountability Office concluded that the available data indicated that there was no additional health risk from reprocessed disposables.

The recycling movement in health care is gaining momentum. More than half of US hospitals send at least some of their plastic equipment for reprocessing. An increasing number of institutions are salvaging unused equipment for donation; that means less medical equipment in landfills and additional cost savings to cash-strapped hospitals. In 2009 the Hospital Corporation of America, which owns 163 hospitals around the country, reported that it had eliminated ninety-four tons of waste through reprocessing.

Reprocessing medical equipment is just one of the subjects examined in the following chapter, which considers strategies to reduce waste and save money. Other topics discussed in the chapter include curbing the use of disposable plastics, plasma gasification, solar-powered trash compactors, and the benefits of single-stream recycling.

"The most powerful thing people can do to clean up the oceans is to refuse to use 'disposable' plastics in the first place."

Eliminating Disposable Plastic Will Decrease Waste

Daniella Russo

Daniella Russo is the executive director of Plastic Pollution Coalition. In the following viewpoint, she accuses human beings of using too much disposable plastic, which is not recycled efficiently and eventually ends up polluting the world's oceans on a massive scale. Russo suggests that individuals change their habits and make a conscious effort to use less disposable plastic in order to save the oceans. She also points out that jobs lost by reducing plastic production can be shifted to industries that produce nontoxic alternatives.

As you read, consider the following questions:

1. According to one estimate, how many pounds of plastic pollution are there in the ocean?

2. What word does the author want to add to the well-known phrase "Reduce, Reuse, Recycle"?

Daniella Russo, "The Other, Bigger 'Oil Spill': Your Use of Disposable Plastic," *Christian Science Monitor*, June 17, 2010. Reproduced by permission of the author.

3. How many people make their living developing and manufacturing plastic, according to the American Chemistry Council (ACC)?

As the world has watched the dreadful string of attempts to stanch the flow of oil from its source a mile down in the Gulf of Mexico, it's a good time to consider ways people can make a positive difference in the ocean.

That petroleum bubbling from the seabed is used to make plastic, and, at an alarming rate, that plastic returns to the ocean as pollution.

We've all been watching the BP [British Petroleum] cam of the broken oil well. But did you know that for quite some time, cameras have logged the swirling gyre in the ocean nicknamed the [Great] Pacific Garbage Patch? Did you know that the environmental devastation of the Atlantic Ocean is not new?

These ocean catastrophes did not begin with a fiery explosion. They began with a disposable cup, just like the cup you likely used at that weekend barbecue.

By one estimate, the ocean has already been corrupted by 200 billion pounds of plastic pollution. Other experts estimate that we are now dumping additional billions of pounds of plastic each year.

Reduce, Reuse, Recycle

The number continues to grow, driven by our ever-increasing consumption of things like plastic toothbrushes, toys, and combs, and single-use items like plastic bags, bottles, and straws.

Whatever happened to that mantra "Reduce, Reuse, Recycle"? Today the recycling part of that has taken off somewhat. But is it too little, too late? A placebo, a myth?

We are simply using too much disposable plastic for the small percentage that gets recycled to even make a dent. And,

"We found it so difficult to reduce our waste, we decided to become horders," cartoon by Grizelda. www.CartoonStock.com. Copyright © Grizelda. Reproduction rights obtainable from www.CartoonStock.com.

unlike paper, glass, or stainless steel, most plastic can only be "down-cycled," or used for increasingly fewer purposes. All the recycling, like using a teaspoon to empty the ocean, simply can't stem the tide of plastic engulfing us.

Billions of pounds of plastic? That's like a few million cars dumped into the sea every year. Maybe we let it happen because the pounds accumulate not by one-ton car increments but by fractions of an ounce—a straw here, a plastic bag there, an empty shampoo bottle over there. When we're doing it one plastic bottle cap at a time, it's hard to realize that we are turning the ocean into a trash can.

Will an Ocean Cleanup Be Effective?

Certainly any effort to clean up our polluted seas is to be applauded, but we should also make sure the work is worth the effort.

In the Gulf of Mexico, the arguably toxic oil-dispersant sprays and containment strategies seem woefully insufficient when barrels of oil churn each day from the source below. Is an ocean cleanup an equally futile effort when we're replacing the garbage that's there more quickly than we could ever scoop it up?

So much of the garbage creating these shameful plastic gyres is single-use disposable plastic.

The most powerful thing people can do to clean up the oceans is to *refuse* to use "disposable" plastics in the first place. Let's add "Refuse" to the list of Rs: Refuse-Reduce-Reuse-Recycle. Until we reduce our use of plastics wherever possible, real change will not happen. Recycling or cleanup projects alone won't cut it.

So what does that mean?

Just Say No to Single-Use Plastic

It means that whenever you can, say no to using plastic that will end up in the garbage that same day. Daily life offers countless ways to start saying no—just start with one.

Once a day, refuse to use a plastic bag, a plastic bottle, straws, takeout containers, disposable cups, utensils, or unnecessary packaging. Start there. Phase out the single-use plastics in your life, reuse the ones you already have as much as you can, and then change your habits: Choose reusable products. Take all of your plastic containers to the nearest recycling center and don't replace them.

Then, begin choosing products sold in glass, metal, cardboard, and paper instead of plastic. These materials can be more effectively recycled or, when it's paper, biodegrade in water or landfills.

What About Jobs in Disposable Plastic?

According to the American Chemistry Council (ACC), roughly 1 million people make a living off developing and manufacturing plastic. But reducing plastic pollution doesn't have to mean reducing jobs.

Members of the ACC who develop plastic should keep jobs by developing new, safe, biodegradable alternatives to plastic that do not leach toxins or contaminate the earth as they biodegrade. Plastic manufacturers should have a plan for the end of life for each of their products and own up to their responsibilities.

Recycling or even reusing alone will not reduce the plastic waste on our planet if we continue to create more and more disposable plastic products every day. As the United States buckles down to months of Gulf oil spill cleanup, we must take advantage of that momentum to save the oceans.

Plastic pollution poses a massive threat to the health of our oceans. If we don't reduce dependence upon and production of single-use plastic alongside that cleanup and recycling, we are engaged in a somewhat Sisyphean [that is, endless] task.

Life without plastic pollution is possible. Try it.

"One thing the world has in abundance is garbage, and the old solution of burying trash in landfills is becoming increasingly expensive as landfills, well, fill up."

Single-Stream Recycling Is Economical and Easy

Kevin Taylor

Kevin Taylor is a writer for the Pacific Northwest Inlander. *In the following viewpoint, he contends that switching to single-stream recycling has been embraced by several Washington State communities. Taylor reports that the most important benefit of the change has been the reduction of the amount of waste going to local landfills, leading also to cost savings. In addition, he cites the innovations in waste handling that have taken place as a result of single-stream recycling.*

As you read, consider the following questions:

1. What kind of recycling does the viewpoint state that Coeur d'Alene communities used before switching to single stream?

Kevin Taylor, "Rethinking Recycling," *Pacific Northwest Inlander*, December 1, 2010. Reproduced by permission.

2. What do officials estimate the waste reduction will be in the amount going to the Fighting Creek landfill by switching to single stream?

3. How many different kinds of recyclables does the viewpoint indicate will be involved in single streaming?

Pop quiz: What was one of the first things to be sold on the international plastics market when Coeur d'Alene [a city in Washington State] changed the way it recycles?

Answer: About 16,000 blue recycling bins.

Yes, the bins. Poof. Gone. "We were flooded with bins. They all came through here," says Steve Moon, plant manager for a local firm that sorts and sells Coeur d'Alene's recyclables. The bins were sold in Canada, which has an active market for many kinds of recycled plastics, he adds.

In mid-October [2010], Coeur d'Alene took a great leap forward into what is known as single-stream recycling, a program that more than doubles the kinds of household items taken for recycling. And it's simple: Everything is dumped into a collection cart that is sorted elsewhere.

The recycling programs locally have long used curbside sorting. Paper, aluminum, plastics are tossed into separate compartments in a specialized truck. Typically, the sorting is slow and limited by the number of compartments on the trucks.

Switching to Single Stream

With single-stream recycling, collection is not limited. Residents toss everything into a wheeled cart—just like a garbage cart, only blue—that is picked up by the same type of truck that collects your trash. The recyclables are taken to a sorting facility, where up to 16 kinds of items can be recovered and sold wherever there is a market. Presently, programs take about six kinds of recyclables.

Waste Management, Coeur d'Alene's garbage collector, recently handed out nearly 16,000 blue 64-gallon wheeled carts, and the program is off to a phenomenal start in just six weeks.

"There is so much material coming in, it's just amazing. Last week we were up to 240,000 pounds—more than double what we were doing before," says Steve Roberge, Coeur d'Alene district manager for Waste Management.

The possibilities of single-stream recycling look so attractive that Waste Management announced earlier this year that it plans to build a sorting facility big enough to handle recyclables from here to Montana.

This was the tipping point, so to speak, for other solid waste collectors, such as the city of Spokane, to begin planning for single stream. One of the drawbacks locally had been lack of a facility to sort the sheer tonnage of recyclables.

Single-stream recycling will be a reality in Spokane by the end of next year or early 2012, says Scott Windsor, director of the city's Solid Waste Management Department.

And not a moment too soon, he says. "Our recycling trucks are about 10 years old. Usually they are replaced after eight," he says. Now that Waste Management is building a sorting facility, Windsor has already budgeted for replacing the aging fleet of recycling trucks with more of the robotic-arm trucks that collect trash.

The same type of cart is used for trash and recyclables.

"All of our customers will get a cart. We are looking at about 70,000," Windsor says.

What's Driving It?

What's driving the change to single stream?

Waste Management in North Idaho spent nearly $1 million, Roberge says, on 16,000 carts and a couple new trucks.

"Our company is an environmental solutions company—that's what we'd like to be known as. Not just garbage," he says. "It doesn't make sense anymore to pick up garbage and bury it in a hole. We want to divert it."

One thing the world has in abundance is garbage, and the old solution of burying trash in landfills is becoming increasingly expensive as landfills, well, fill up.

It costs $450,000 to prepare and fill an acre with trash at Kootenai County's Fighting Creek landfill, and then another $190,000 to close it. Single-stream recycling is expected to reduce waste going to Fighting Creek by 30 to 50 percent.

"The benefit to the county is we are not running this to the landfill. That is a shared benefit to everybody when the landfill's life is extended," says Steve Wulf, principal planner for Kootenai County Solid Waste.

Even in Spokane, Windsor says, "The waste-to-energy plant has two burners and it processes 270,000 to 280,000 tons a year—it burns anything and everything."

But the city still ships between 60,000 to 70,000 tons of trash to the Rabanco regional landfill near Goldendale, Wash.

"Anything we can divert as recycling . . . there will be savings," Windsor says.

What Goes In

"My figures show we are up 166 percent from the blue-bin system," says Wulf.

The new carts take 16 kinds of recyclables, Wulf says, including an expanded range of plastics and papers.

In addition to plastic beverage bottles, Coeur d'Alene residents can now recycle plastic detergent containers, the crinkly clear plastic that many foods and baked goods come in.

Single stream won't take plastic bags (they get snagged in machinery), PVC pipes or Styrofoam, Wulf says.

"We also ask people to stay away from [recycling] motor oil and pesticide containers," Wulf says.

Other new recyclables include cereal boxes and junk mail, says Waste Management's Roberge. What stays out? Glass, all three Steves (Wulf, Roberge and Moon) say. There is no market for it, and Coeur d'Alene is not collecting it.

"One caveat I have for the people of Coeur d'Alene: It would be really great if they would keep their glass and their garbage out," says Moon of Spokane Recycling. "We get diapers, we get electronic components, old printers, old you-name-its, old stereos and old spoiled food. The guys work hard enough without having to handle things that shouldn't be there."

Wulf says some hard-core homeowners think that if they put glass in the blue carts, someone down the line will find a way to recycle it.

Not so, says Moon. "It goes right into a dump."

Confusion with food waste may arise from Spokane's recent decision to accept some food scraps in the "clean and green" bins for composting. Food should not go into the blue carts.

And diapers . . . "Ohhhh," says Moon.

'Nuf said.

Where It Comes Out

Everyone interviewed for this [viewpoint] noted the recycled commodities markets are volatile and unpredictable.

The nice thing about sorting out a wide array of items is that a strong market can support weaker ones.

"We follow the pricing monthly," says Moon of Spokane Recycling. "It goes up and down, but it's OK. It's end-user driven: If not a lot of people are reading newspapers, then newsprint is down; if people aren't buying a lot of Wal-Mart or other big-box store packages, then cardboard is down.

"It follows the economy pretty closely," he says.

Some markets are practically next door. Newspaper goes to the Inland Empire paper mill in Millwood.

Three to five semi loads full of cardboard pull out of Spokane Recycling every day, bound for a customer in Oregon.

Plastics often go to Canada and China, as more and more manufacturers around the world use recycled products, Moon says.

The company's Coeur d'Alene plant, Bluebird Recycling, is being expanded and upgraded with new sorting machinery to handle the increased tonnage, Moon says.

Right now he has a crew of nine who handle the 10 to 12 tons a day shipped over from Coeur d'Alene. "It keeps us hopping."

Technologically Advanced Processing

The new sorting machinery is pretty Rube Goldbergian [a machine with a complex design that performs a simple task], as Moon and the city of Spokane's Windsor describe it.

"There are machines that optically sort stuff by color. There's compressed air" to blow away lighter items, Windsor says.

"You've got angled belts where, as the material drops onto them, the heavier parts roll downhill into conveyors that carry them off," Moon adds.

The idea behind all these shaking and whizzing belts is to turn something old into something new and try to find less offensive ways to deal with waste.

"I do think it is a growth industry . . . and single stream makes it a lot easier. As people understand it more, I hope they utilize it to the max. It's good for them and it's good for the environment," Moon says.

> *"Instead of spending money driving trucks around—burning gas and spewing carbon dioxide into the ozone— we'd all be better served spending the same money on efficiency-producing compactors."*

Solar-Powered Trash Compactors Can Make Trash Collection More Efficient

Daniel Gross

Daniel Gross is a writer for Slate.com. In the following viewpoint, he maintains that solar-powered trash compactors are more efficient than current popular methods of collecting garbage because compactors enable trucks to pick up more garbage in fewer trips. Gross elucidates the environmental advantages of using solar-powered trash compactors, starting with fewer trucks on the streets and using clean energy. He also touts the economic advantages of increasing efficiencies in waste management that he claims offset the start-up costs involved.

As you read, consider the following questions:

1. By how much does the viewpoint indicate BigBelly Solar's sales rose in 2009?

2. When does Gross report that the first solar-powered trash compactor was sold?

3. How much does a BigBelly unit cost, according to Gross?

If you had to devise a product designed to succeed in this unique climate, it might be one that makes an eco-friendly, alternative-energy-powered, carbon-reducing, American-made, public-space-beautifying commodity that saves municipalities money and that can be purchased with stimulus funds.

In other words, it might be the BigBelly [Solar] solar-powered trash compactor. Capital investment and discretionary spending have fallen this year [2009], but BigBelly's sales are up 80 percent.

An Inefficient Process

Early this decade, company founder Jim Poss, who had worked in the solar and electric vehicle fields, was struck by the number of overflowing garbage cans he saw and the huge inefficiencies he detected in the carting business. Garbage cans are filled mostly with air and the trucks are expensive to operate—about $100 per hour, all costs considered. "I figured there's a lot of inefficiency there. If you compact trash on site, you can make trucks and the people running them more effective." Instead of spending money driving trucks around— burning gas and spewing carbon dioxide into the ozone— we'd all be better served spending the same money on efficiency-producing compactors. Especially if those compactors keep streets clean by trapping garbage inside them and can be powered by a free source of clean energy: the sun.

Poss started the company while getting his MBA at Babson College. A solar panel on the top of the container charges a battery, and when volume reaches a certain level, it starts compacting with 1,200 pounds of force, providing a 5-to-1 reduction in volume. "On a busy day, it'll run for 15 minutes," says Poss. Since the compactor fills up more slowly than a garbage can, it doesn't need to be emptied as often, which makes it a potential money-saver when used in remote areas—like ski resorts and state parks—or in urban areas where volumes of trash require frequent pickups. Funded by angel investors at first, Poss has raised about $10 million in capital. He contracted with a firm in Vermont to manufacture the BigBelly and sold his first machine to Vail Resorts in early 2004.

Although it is made in America, BigBelly is reminiscent of a futuristic Japanese robot. Flashing lights indicate when it is full and needs to be emptied. Many are wireless enabled, which effectively turns them into Twitterers—they transmit brief text messages to a centralized Web site to let owners know when compactors are full. Like many smart green products, they're not cheap—and they're much more expensive than the dumb product they're hoping to dislodge. It costs about $80 a month to lease a BigBelly, or from $3,000 to $3,900 to purchase one, though those buying in bulk get a discount.

The Savings

As a rule of thumb, Poss says, if the installation of a BigBelly can save an hour of collection time per month on a garbage can, it pays off relatively quickly. "In a city that collects once per day, or in a park system where there's travel time of 10 to 20 minutes to reach a garbage can and they collect three times per week," it pays for itself in about three to four years. For a large-scale user who deploys them in a concentrated area, the savings can be greater. Earlier this year, Philadelphia leased 500 BigBellys and placed them downtown. In areas where the

The Success of BigBelly Solar

In the short term, the ruthless pursuit of efficiency translates into the uncomfortable—and unsustainable—dichotomy of rising profits and falling employment. But the focus on efficiency is creating new business opportunities for smart companies. At BigBelly Solar, a Needham, Mass.-based firm whose solar-powered trash compactors reduce the need for both labor and energy, sales doubled in both 2008 and 2009. "Cities and institutions like universities and park systems are eager to do more with less," says CEO [chief executive officer] Jim Poss. Leasing 500 compacting units has allowed Philadelphia to cut weekly pickups from 17 to five, and will save it $13 million over 10 years. BigBelly employs fewer than 50 people, but like many businesses in fast-growing markets it indirectly supports a much larger number of jobs.

Daniel Gross, "The Comeback Country,"
Newsweek, *April 9, 2010.*

BigBelly operates, the city picks up the trash five times per week instead of 17. Poss says the city is saving $800,000 a year in labor and fuel costs and will save $12 million over the products' 10-year life span—without any reduction in service. Philadelphia has redeployed workers from collecting trash to recycling initiatives. "It's not a solution for every trash can in the world, but it is one for millions of trash cans in the U.S.," says Poss.

The Future of BigBelly

BigBelly is still more like a start-up than an industrial giant. So far, the company has sold more than 3,000 units, with sales of 2,000 expected this year alone. Other areas of BigBelly concentration include Boston (more than 200) and Massachusetts state parks (about 100). BigBelly employs 24 people, and Poss says the company has "recently had a couple of profitable months." In June, BigBelly partnered with trash-removal giant Waste Management to sell compactors.

Like the compact fluorescent lightbulb, BigBelly compactors are expensive replacements that can justify their high costs through savings generated over time, even in the absence of government incentives. But Poss anticipates that the stimulus bill may help. One challenge to adoption is that already pinched municipal budgets generally maintain separate line items for trucks, for collection, and for trash cans. But the BigBelly doesn't fit neatly into any of those. The flow of funds to states and municipalities, Poss notes, has given potential purchasers more flexibility to make investments that yield savings.

BigBelly is still a very small company, and the solar-powered compactors it has placed into service amount to a few biodegradable packages placed on top of a landfill. But its progress signifies a truism about this post-bubble economy: Efficiency is the new growth. In this period of universally tight budgets, products and services—even expensive ones—that demonstrate an ability to save resources and money are gaining traction. Said Poss: "People who were receptive to us because we're green are now really receptive to us because we save money, and, by the way, we're also green."

| "Beyond the limits of the human eye another world exists."

Electrobiochemical Reactors Treat Waste Efficiently and Cheaply

Brendon Bosworth

Brendon Bosworth is a writer for NewWest.net, an online news source. In the following viewpoint, he explores the promising field of electrobiochemical reactor (EBR) technology, a process that cleans contaminated mining wastewater using microbes and a constant stream of electrons. Bosworth reports that EBR can also be used to clean agricultural, industrial, and oil-production wastewater and is inexpensive enough to be used in a broad range of countries. He also indicates that the potential for further and more widespread applications of this technology is enormous.

As you read, consider the following questions:

1. How does the cost of EBR compare with filtration or precipitation, according to Bosworth?

2. How much does the viewpoint state that EBR technology costs per one thousand gallons of water processed?

Brendon Bosworth, "Utah Scientists Harness Electrons for Better Wastewater Cleaning," NewWest.net, January 14, 2011. Reproduced by permission.

3. According to the viewpoint, how much water can a full-scale EBR system process per minute?

Beyond the limits of the human eye another world exists. Microbes, tiny single-cell organisms, inhabit pretty much every environment on the planet, even extreme ones like the scalding springs at Yellowstone National Park. From plankton in the ocean to salmonella lurking on sketchy food, they are powerful determinants of what happens in our realm.

Electrobiochemical Technology

The microscopic domain of certain highly useful microbes is well known by Jack Adams, a metallurgical engineering research professor at the University of Utah and president of start-up company Inotec. Along with company co-founder Mike Peoples, a doctoral student in environmental engineering, he has refined a method for cleaning contaminated mining wastewater that uses microbes and a steady stream of electrons.

It's called an electrobiochemical reactor (or EBR) and Adams says it can save the mining industry a lot of money. It can also make clean drinking water cheaply available for those living in impoverished parts of the globe, Peoples says.

Benefits of EBR

"We're working with NGOs [nongovernmental organizations] from India and Bangladesh for humanitarian purposes, because a lot of drinking water around the world has heavy metal poisoning," he says. "We work with industry and humanitarian type companies as well."

"What's good is there's not a lot of moving parts," he says. "Once you get the bugs established, and you take good care of them, it's a fairly cheap process compared to filtration or precipitation, which makes it viable for small villages in rural areas in [places] like India and China that can use it as a pretreatment step in removing their heavy metals, which is a big issue."

Mining firms use a variety of methods to clean the tons of toxic wastewater they produce, which is laden with heavy metals such as arsenic and mercury. These include filtering the liquid through semipermeable membranes, in what is known as ultrafiltration, as well as reverse osmosis.

Foul water can also be dosed with chemicals and nutrients, which stimulate waterborne microbes to remove contaminants, or compounds such as lime to precipitate metals. But this is not always efficient or cost-effective, according to Adams.

He says reverse osmosis and membrane filtration can cost from a few dollars to more than $10 per 1,000 gallons of water processed, while conventional biological processes can cost between $1 and $3 per thousand gallons.

By comparison, the patented EBR technology reduces costs to about 25 cents per 1,000 gallons, he says.

How It Works

When electrons are added to the EBR system they fuel the activity of waterborne microbes that work to remove metals.

"All biological and chemical reactions require the addition or removal of electrons," Adams says. He explains that when excess chemicals and nutrients are added into a conventional reactor, microbes will take electrons from them, but the microbes have to work harder to get this source of energy. This is because the microbes first need to break apart the bonds between carbon molecules to release the electrons.

To make things easier for the microbes and help them do their removal job faster, the scientists feed them a steady supply of electrons. Instead of preparing a home-cooked meal the hard way, the microbes now hit the drive-through. Just one volt supplies one trillion trillion electrons. (That's not a typo, just a huge number.)

"We replace literally tons of chemicals over the life span of the reactor operation with a small amount of electricity," Adams says.

Adams says a full-scale EBR system, which could process an average of 600 gallons per minute, can run off a small solar grid. While doing their laboratory tests, the researchers have been using the voltage required to power a small flashlight. "It's the same type of charge you would use in your solar backpack system to charge the appliances you might take into the backcountry," Adams says.

To harvest the best microbes for the job the researchers look for microbes already living in the contaminated area, so they're used to the environment. Those that specifically remove the required contaminants are grown to high concentrations, while being fed on affordable sources of carbon, such as molasses, Peoples explains. Once ready, the colony is placed in the reactor where they attach to a layer of pumice.

The Potential of EBR

Adams and Peoples have performed laboratory tests on wastewater from major mines in Utah, Wyoming, Colorado, Montana and Canada, successfully removing selenium, arsenic, mercury, and inorganic materials including nitrates and sulfates. Adams says the technology can be used to clean agricultural, industrial and oil-production wastewater, but for now their focus is on mining.

With support from the University of Utah's Technology Commercialization Office—which assists faculty with start-up endeavors—and the mining industry, Inotec is gathering momentum just one year into operation. The company recently tied up its first pilot-scale contract, treating wastewater from an inactive gold mine. It has landed a second pilot-scale test at a mine for silver and other metals in the Yukon. Last year [2010], Adams and Peoples won the Rocky Mountain regional award at the Cleantech Open competition in San Jose, California.

Depending on the required level of water purity, the EBR can be used alone or in conjunction with other filtration steps. "For environmental discharge it might be able to be used alone and produce high enough quality water to feed trout fisheries or something like that," Adams says. "But if you're using it for drinking water you would want an additional step or two so that the water doesn't contain the microbes that are growing in the EBR."

Adams says EBR produces "thousands of times less" sludge than conventional reactors, which create sludge that generally has to be disposed of as hazardous waste. "The material formed is in such a state that it can be recycled to offset some of the treatment costs," he says. "We're reducing pollution on both ends."

Peoples points out that mining is already intensive on water use, but will likely become even more so in the future, as the concentrations of available ores in rock diminish. "The issue of water treatment and mining is only going to increase in time, due to the issue of deposits becoming harder to find and extract. All the easy stuff is gone."

A Revolution

Peoples says modern microbial research is part of a revolution. "In the last twenty years this science has really blossomed. We're just scratching the surface. Twenty years ago they put a whole new branch into the tree of life, called archaea."

"It's really exciting, but what's even better is it's applied. I'm going out and putting in these new systems. . . . It's like an adventure."

| "Called plasma gasification, it works a little like the big bang, only backward (you get nothing from something)."

Plasma Gasification Successfully Converts Trash into Energy

Michael Behar

Michael Behar is a writer for Popular Science. *In the following viewpoint, he investigates the potential of plasma gasification to reduce waste and turn it into energy. Behar enumerates the benefits of the plasma-gasification process, which breaks down almost anything into a synthesis gas that can be converted into a range of marketable fuels. The author anticipates the possibilities for broader use of plasma gasification to reduce costs for municipalities as large as New York City, but notes that the process has critics who question the ecological impact of its by-products on water supplies.*

As you read, consider the following questions:

1. How much waste does the viewpoint indicate a Startech machine could handle per day?

Michael Behar, "The Prophet of Garbage," *Popular Science*, March 1, 2007. Reproduced by permission.

2. If New York City were using plasma-gasification plants to get rid of two thousand tons of garbage a day, how much would it cost per day, according to Behar?

3. How much does Behar state that it is costing New York City to get rid of its trash per year?

It sounds as if someone just dropped a tricycle into a meat grinder. I'm sitting inside a narrow conference room at a research facility in Bristol, Connecticut, chatting with Joseph Longo, the founder and CEO of Startech Environmental Corporation. As we munch on takeout Subway sandwiches, a plate-glass window is the only thing separating us from the adjacent lab, which contains a glowing caldera of "plasma" three times as hot as the surface of the sun. Every few minutes there's a horrific clanking noise—grinding followed by a thunderous voomp, like the sound a gas barbecue makes when it first ignites.

"Is it supposed to do that?" I ask Longo nervously. "Yup," he says. "That's normal."

An Introduction to the Plasma Converter

Despite his 74 years, Longo bears an unnerving resemblance to the longtime cover boy of *Mad* magazine, Alfred E. Neuman, who shrugs off nuclear Armageddon with the glib catchphrase "What, me worry?" Both share red hair, a smattering of freckles and a toothy grin. When such a man tells me I'm perfectly safe from a 30,000°F arc of man-made lightning heating a vat of plasma that his employees are "controlling" in the next room—well, I'm not completely reassured.

To put me at ease, Longo calls in David Lynch, who manages the demonstration facility. "There's no flame or fire inside. It's just electricity," Lynch assures me of the multimillion-dollar system that took Longo almost two decades to design and build. Then the two usher me into the lab, where the gleaming 15-foot-tall machine they've named the Plasma Converter stands in the center of the room. The entire thing takes up about as much space as a two-car garage, surprisingly compact for a machine that can consume nearly any type of waste—from dirty diapers to chemical weapons—by annihilating toxic materials in a process as old as the universe itself.

Plasma Gasification

Called plasma gasification, it works a little like the big bang, only backward (you get nothing from something). Inside a sealed vessel made of stainless steel and filled with a stable gas—either pure nitrogen or, as in this case, ordinary air—a 650-volt current passing between two electrodes rips electrons from the air, converting the gas into plasma. Current flows continuously through this newly formed plasma, creating a field of extremely intense energy very much like lightning. The radiant energy of the plasma arc is so powerful, it disintegrates trash into its constituent elements by tearing apart molecular bonds. The system is capable of breaking down pretty much anything except nuclear waste, the isotopes of which are indestructible. The only by-products are an obsidian-like glass used as a raw material for numerous applications, including bathroom tiles and high-strength asphalt, and a synthesis gas, or "syngas"—a mixture of primarily hydrogen and carbon monoxide that can be converted into a variety of marketable fuels, including ethanol, natural gas and hydrogen.

Perhaps the most amazing part of the process is that it's self-sustaining. Just like your toaster, Startech's Plasma Converter draws its power from the electrical grid to get started. The initial voltage is about equal to the zap from a police stun gun. But once the cycle is under way, the 2,200°F syngas is fed into a cooling system, generating steam that drives turbines to produce electricity. About two-thirds of the power is siphoned off to run the converter; the rest can be used on-site for heating or electricity, or sold back to the utility grid. "Even a blackout would not stop the operation of the facility," Longo says.

It all sounds far too good to be true. But the technology works. Over the past decade, half a dozen companies have been developing plasma technology to turn garbage into energy. "The best renewable energy is the one we complain about the most: municipal solid waste," says Louis Circeo, the director of plasma research at the Georgia Institute of Technology. "It will prove cheaper to take garbage to a plasma plant than it is to dump it on a landfill." A Startech machine that costs roughly $250 million could handle 2,000 tons of waste daily, approximately what a city of a million people amasses in that time span. Large municipalities typically haul their trash to landfills, where the operator charges a "tipping fee" to dump the waste. The national average is $35 a ton, although the cost can be more than twice that in the Northeast (where land is scarce, tipping fees are higher). And the tipping fee a city pays doesn't include the price of trucking the garbage often hundreds of miles to a landfill or the cost of capturing leaky methane—a greenhouse gas—from the decomposing waste. In a city with an average tipping fee, a $250-million converter could pay for itself in about 10 years, and that's without factoring in the money made from selling the excess electricity and syngas. After that break-even point, it's pure profit.

Someday very soon, cities might actually make money from garbage.

Talking Trash

It was a rainy morning when I pulled up to Startech R&D [research and development] to see Longo waiting for me in the parking lot. Wearing a bright yellow oxford shirt, a striped tie and blue pinstriped pants, he dashed across the blacktop to greet me as I stepped from my rental car. A street-smart Brooklyn native, Longo was an only child raised by parents who worked long hours at a local factory that made baseballs and footballs. He volunteered to fight in Korea as a paratrooper after a friend was killed in action. He's fond of antiquated slang like "attaboy" and "shills" (as in "those shills stole my patents") and is old-school enough to have only recently abandoned the protractors, pencils and drafting tables that he used to design his original Plasma Converter in favor of computers.

Today, Longo is meeting with investors from U.S. Energy, a trio of veteran waste-disposal executives who recently formed a partnership to build the first plasma-gasification plant on Long Island, New York. They own a transfer station (where garbage goes for sorting en route to landfills) and are in the process of buying six Startech converters to handle 3,000 tons of construction debris a day trucked from sites around the state. "It's mostly old tile, wood, nails, glass, metal and wire all mixed together," one of the project's partners, Troy Caruso, tells me. For the demonstration, Longo prepares a sampling of typical garbage—bottles of leftover prescription drugs, bits of fiberglass insulation, a half-empty can of Slim-Fast. A conveyer belt feeds the trash into an auger, which shreds and crushes it into pea-size morsels (that explains the deafening grinding sound) before stuffing it into the plasma-reactor chamber. The room is warm and humid, and a dull hum emanates from the machinery.

Caruso and his partners, Paul Marazzo and Michael Nuzzi, are silent at first. They've seen the demo before. But as more trash vanishes into the converter, they become increasingly animated, spouting off facts and figures about how the machine will revolutionize their business. "This technology eliminates the landfill, which is 80 percent of our costs," Nuzzi says. "And we can use it to generate fuel at the back end," adds Marazzo, who then asks Lynch if the converter can handle chunks of concrete (answer: yes). "The bottom line is that nobody wants a landfill in their backyard," Nuzzi tells me. New York City is already paying an astronomical $90 a ton to get rid of its trash. According to Startech, a few 2,000-ton-per-day plasma-gasification plants could do it for $36. Sell the syngas and surplus electricity, and you'd actually net $15 a ton. "Gasification is not just environmentally friendly," Nuzzi says. "It's a good business decision."

The converter we're watching vaporize Slim-Fast is a mini version of Startech's technology, capable of consuming five tons a day of solid waste, or about what 2,200 Americans toss in the trash every 24 hours. Fueled with garbage from the local dump, the converter is fired up whenever Longo pitches visiting clients.

A Rising Technology

Longo has been talking with the National Science Foundation about installing a system at McMurdo Station in Antarctica. The Vietnamese government is considering buying one to get rid of stockpiles of Agent Orange that the U.S. military left behind after the war. Investors from China, Poland, Japan, Romania, Italy, Russia, Brazil, Venezuela, the U.K., Mexico and Canada have all entered contract negotiations with Startech after making the pilgrimage to Bristol to see Longo's dog-and-pony show.

Startech isn't the only company using plasma to turn waste into a source of clean energy. A handful of start-ups—Geoplasma, Recovered Energy, PyroGenesis [Canada], EnviroArc and Plasco Energy, among others—have entered the market in the past decade. But Longo, who has worked in the garbage business for four decades, is perhaps the industry's most passionate founding father. "What's so devilishly wonderful about plasma gasification is that it's completely circular," he says. "It takes everything back to its fundamental components in a way that's beautiful." Although all plasma-gasification systems recapture syngas to turn into fuel, Startech's "Starcell" system seems to be ahead of the pack in its ability to economically convert the substance into eco-friendly and competitively priced fuels. "A lot of other gasification technologies require multiple steps. This is a one-step process," says Patrick Davis

What Is Plasma Gasification?

A waste treatment technology that uses intense electrical energy and the high temperature created by an electrical arc to break down waste material into its basic molecular structure.

Alliance Federated Energy,
"Why Plasma Gasification? Environmental FAQ," 2010.

of the U.S. Department of Energy's office of hydrogen production and delivery, which has awarded Longo's company almost $1 million in research grants. "You put the waste in the reactor and you get out the syngas. That's it."

The Garbage Man

After his tour of duty in Korea, Longo put himself through night school at the Brooklyn Polytechnic Institute. In 1959, engineering degree in hand, he got a job at American Machine & Foundry (AMF)—the same company that today runs the world's largest chain of bowling alleys—designing hardened silos for nuclear intercontinental ballistic missiles, such as Titan and Minuteman. "There was never a time I can remember when I didn't want to be an engineer," he says.

For years, Longo tried to convince his bosses at AMF to go into the garbage business (as manager of new product development, he was charged with investigating growth areas). "I knew a lot about the industry, how backward it was," he says. The costs to collect and transport waste were climbing. He was sure there had to be a better way.

In 1967 Longo quit his job at AMF to start his own business, called International Dynetics. The name might not be familiar, but its product should: Longo designed and built the world's first industrial-size trash compactors. "If you live in a high-rise or apartment building and dump your trash down a chute," he says, "it's probably going into one of our compactors."

When Longo started his company, it was still easier and cheaper to just haul the loose trash to the dump. But gas prices climbed, inflation increased, and soon, business boomed. In a few years, there were thousands of International Dynetics compactors operating around the world. The machines could crush the equivalent of five 30-gallon cans crammed with trash into a cube that was about the size of a small television. "Our purpose was to condense it so it would be easier and cost less to bring to a landfill," he says.

Then, in 1972, Longo read a paper in a science journal about fusion reactors. "The authors speculated that plasma might be used to destroy waste to the elemental level someday in the future," he recalls. "That was like a spear in the heart, because we had just got our patents out for our trash compactors, and these guys were already saying there's a prettier girl coming to town," he says. "It would make obsolete everything we were doing. I resisted looking at the technology for 10 years. But by 1984, it became obvious that plasma could do some serious work."

By then, the principal component of today's plasma-gasification systems, the plasma torch, had become widespread in the metal-fabrication industry, where it is used as a cutting knife for slicing through slabs of steel. Most engineers at the time were focused on ways to improve plasma torches for manipulating metals. But Longo had trash on the brain—whole landfills of trash. He was intent on developing a system that used plasma to convert waste into energy on a large scale. So he jumped ship again. In 1988 Longo sold International Dynetics and founded Startech.

Plasma to the People

"People kept asking me, 'If this is so good, Longo, then why isn't everyone already using one?'" he says, referring to himself in the third person, a device he relies on frequently to emphasize his point. "We had the technical capability, but we didn't have a product yet. Just because we could do the trick didn't mean it was worth doing." Trucking garbage to dumps and landfills was still cheap. Environmental concerns weren't on the public radar the way they are today, and landfills and incinerators weren't yet widely seen as public menaces. "We outsourced the parts to build our first converter," Longo says. "When we told the manufacturers we were working with plasma, some of them thought it had something to do with blood and AIDS."

Longo describes the development curve as "relentless." He teamed up with another engineer who had experience in the waste industry and an interest in plasma technology. "We didn't have computers. We did everything on drafting boards. But I was aggressive. And the more we did, the more it compelled us to continue." It took almost a decade of R&D until they had a working prototype.

"I felt like St. Peter bringing the message out," Longo says of his first sales calls. In 1997 the U.S. Army became Startech's inaugural customer, buying a converter to dispose of chemical weapons at the Aberdeen Proving Ground in Maryland. A second reactor went to Japan for processing polychlorinated biphenyls, or PCBs, an industrial coolant and lubricant banned in the U.S since 1977 ("really nasty stuff," Longo says).

Longo realized early on that what would make plasma gasification marketable was a machine that could handle anything. Some of the most noxious chemicals, he knew from his decades in the garbage industry, are found in the most mundane places, like household solid waste. Startech has an edge over some of its competitors because its converter doesn't have to be reconfigured for different materials, which means operators don't have to presort waste, a costly and time-consuming process. To achieve this adaptability, Startech converters crank the plasma arc up to an extremely high operating temperature: 30,000°F. Getting that temperature just right was one of Longo's key developmental challenges. "You can't rely on the customer to tell you what they put in," Longo says. "Sometimes they don't know, sometimes they lie, and sometimes they've thrown in live shotgun shells from a hunting trip. That's why it's imperative that the Plasma Converter can take in anything."

A video camera mounted near the top of the converter at the Bristol plant gives me a glimpse of the plasma arc doing its dirty work. At a computer station near the converter, Lynch taps a few commands into a keyboard, and a loud hiss fills the room, the sound of steam being released from behind a pressurized valve. "You can use that steam to heat your facility and neighboring buildings," he says proudly. Next to him is an LCD monitor with a live video feed from inside the reactor. A vivid magenta glow fills the screen as I watch the plasma torch vaporize a bucket of cell phones and soda cans. A hopper at the top of the vessel dumps another load into the plasma reactor, and seconds later, it vanishes too. "The idea," Lynch says, "is that regardless of what you put in the front end, what comes out will be clean and ready to use for whatever you want." I've watched him operate the converter for nearly an hour, and I'm still stunned to see no smoke, no flames, no ash, no pollution of any kind—all that's left is syngas, the fuel source, and the molten obsidian-like material.

Catching the Litter Bug

Low transportation costs, cheap land, weak environmental regulations—these factors help explain why it took plasma until now to catch on as an economically sensible strategy to dispose of waste. "The steep increase in energy prices over the past two years is what has made this technology viable," says

Hilburn Hillestad, president of Geoplasma. His company, which touts the slogan "waste destruction at the speed of lightning with energy to share," is negotiating a deal with St. Lucie County, Florida, to erect a $425-million plasma-gasification system near a local landfill. The plant in St. Lucie County will be large enough to devour all 2,000 tons of daily trash generated by the county *and* polish off an additional 1,000 tons a day from the old landfill. Of course, the technology, still unproven on a large scale, has its skeptics. "That obsidian-like slag contains toxic heavy metals and breaks down when exposed to water," claims Brad van Guilder, a scientist at the Ecology Center in Ann Arbor, Michigan, which advocates for clean air and water. "Dump it in a landfill, and it could one day contaminate local groundwater." Others wonder about the cleanliness of the syngas. "In the cool-down phases, the components in the syngas could reform into toxins," warns Monica Wilson, the international coordinator for the Global Alliance for Incinerator Alternatives, in Berkeley, California. None of this seems to worry St. Lucie County's solid-waste director, Leo Cordeiro. "We'll get all our garbage to disappear, and our landfill will be gone in 20 years," he tells me. The best part: Geoplasma is footing the entire bill. "We'll generate 160 megawatts a day from the garbage," Hillestad says, "but we'll consume only 40 megawatts to run the plant. We'll sell the net energy to the local power grid." Sales from excess electricity might allow Geoplasma to break even in 20 years.

In New York, Carmen Cognetta, an attorney with the city council's infrastructure division, is evaluating how plasma gasification could help offset some of the city's exorbitant waste costs. "All the landfills around New York have closed, incinerators are banned, and we are trucking our trash to Virginia and Pennsylvania," he explains. "That is costing the city $400 million a year. We could put seven or eight of these converters in the city, and that would be enough." The syngas from the converters, Cognetta says, could be tapped for hydrogen gas to power buses or police cars. But the decision-making bureaucracy can be slow, and it is hamstrung by the politically well-connected waste-disposal industry. "Many landfill operators are used to getting a million dollars a month out of debris," says U.S. Energy's Paul Marazzo. "They don't want a converter to happen because they'll lose their revenue."

Anticipation for Hydrogen Boom

Meanwhile, Victor Sziky, the president of Sicmar International, an investment firm based in Panama, is working with the Panamanian government to set up at least 10 Startech systems there. "The garbage problem here is exploding in conjunction with growth," says Sziky, who lives in Panama City. "We have obsolete incinerators, and landfills that are polluting groundwater and drinking water. We've had outbreaks of cholera and hepatitis A and B directly attributed to the waste in landfills. There are a lot of people in a small country, and there's no infrastructure to deal with it." The project will be capable of destroying 200 tons of trash a day at each location, enough to handle all the garbage for the municipalities involved—and, says Sziky, to produce up to 40 percent of their electrical demand.

Panama's syngas will probably be converted to hydrogen and sold to industrial suppliers. The current market for hydrogen is at least $50 billion worldwide, a figure that is expected to grow by 5 to 10 percent annually, according to the National Hydrogen Association, an industry and research consortium. Analysts at Fuji-Keizai USA, a market-research firm for emerging technologies, predict that the domestic market will hit $1.6 billion by 2010, up from $800 million in 2005. The Department of Energy's Patrick Davis says that when the long-awaited hydrogen-powered vehicles finally arrive, the demand for hydrogen will soar. But he also notes that to have an effect on global warming, it's critical that hydrogen come from clean sources.

That's one more idea that's old news to Longo, who, as usual, is 10 steps ahead of the game, already embedded in a future where fossil fuels are artifacts of a bygone era. For the past several years, he has been developing the Starcell, a filtration mechanism that slaps onto the back end of his converter and quickly refines syngas into hydrogen. As he says, "We are the disruptive technology." Longo has been working in garbage for 40 years, making his fortune by literally scraping the bottom of the barrel. Which is, it turns out, the perfect vantage point for finding new ways to turn what to most of us is just garbage into arguably the most valuable thing in the world: clean energy.

"Health care can contribute to creating a livable planet by reducing the substantial amount of medical waste it produces."

Reprocessing Medical Equipment Minimizes Waste and Saves Money

Gifty Kwakye, Peter Pronovost, and Martin A. Makary

Gifty Kwakye is a medical student; Peter Pronovost is a professor at Johns Hopkins University School of Medicine; and Martin A. Makary is chair of gastrointestinal surgery at Johns Hopkins University School of Medicine and associate professor in the Johns Hopkins Center for Global Health. In the following viewpoint, the authors contend that the reprocessing of medical equipment is a cost-effective way to reduce the amount of waste produced by health care providers and to reduce costs. Kwakye, Pronovost, and Makary argue that the practice has a reliable safety record and is worthy of serious consideration. The authors also make recommendations for the oversight of equipment re-

Gifty Kwakye, Peter Pronovost, and Martin A. Makary, "A Call to Go Green in Health Care by Reprocessing Medical Equipment," *Journal of the Association of American Medical Colleges*, vol. 85, March 2010, pp. 398–400. Reproduced by permission.

processing for academic medical centers and indicate that educating staff and students prior to implementing the program will yield the best results.

As you read, consider the following questions:

1. How much medical waste do American health care facilities dispose of every year, according to the viewpoint?

2. What percentage of hospitals does the viewpoint indicate use reprocessing?

3. According to the authors, what percentage of large hospitals reprocess their medical equipment?

Abstract

Health care is one of the largest contributors to waste production in the United States. Given increased awareness of the environmental and financial costs associated with waste disposal and its public health impact, many hospitals are adopting environmentally friendly practices that reduce waste production and offer equally effective, yet less expensive alternatives. Reprocessing of medical equipment is one such practice that has gained popularity in recent years and has led to major cost savings across several medical disciplines. In this commentary, we seek to take a closer look at the practice of reprocessing, explore the evidence surrounding its safety, and suggest implications of reprocessing for medical centers.

Bipartisan policy leaders have proposed the adoption of "green" energy and technology as one solution to the widespread economic crisis. Going green on a national level has been projected both to reduce long-term federal spending and to support environmental goals of sustainability. Although many health care providers have been strong proponents for environmentally conscious practices, it is estimated that American health care facilities continue to dispose of over four billion pounds of waste annually in landfills and commercial incinerators, making the health industry the second-largest contributor to landfills after the food industry.[1] Medical schools and teaching hospitals, which make up approximately 22% of U.S. hospitals, also contribute their fair share to health care waste.

One relatively new green practice receiving much attention is the reprocessing of medical equipment.[2] Already, more than 25% of U.S. hospitals, including our institution, are using reprocessing as a means of decreasing the tons of disposable waste generated annually.[3] We have found it to be a common-sense strategy that uses detailed quality-control standards to recalibrate, clean, sterilize, and remanufacture medical equipment. The result has been a significant waste reduction and cost savings. However, uptake of such green practices by hospitals has continued to be slow because of a misunderstanding of the process and concerns about patient safety. In this commentary, we attempt to address these barriers by explaining what reprocessing is, exploring its history and economic benefits, and reviewing the evidence regarding its safety. Finally, we look at the implications of this green process on academic medical centers (AMCs).

What Is Reprocessing?

The American Society for Healthcare Central Service Professionals describes reprocessing as any process which renders a used, reusable, or single-use device (SUD) to be patient-ready or which allows an unused product that has been opened to be made patient-ready.[4] According to the U.S. Food and Drug Administration (FDA), a SUD is any device intended for one use or on a single patient, whereas a reprocessed SUD is an original device that has previously been used on a patient and has been subjected to additional processing and manufacturing for the purpose of additional use on a patient.[5]

As in all activities, incentives—both economic and non-economic—drive behavior. Before the introduction of SUDs, most medical devices were manufactured for multiple uses and were reused after cleaning and sterilization by locally trained hospital staff. With increasing concerns regarding safety and rising costs of sterilizing multiple-use devices, health care migrated to SUDs. But as these also became increasingly sophisticated, their costs drove health care organizations to explore other options such as reprocessing which was conducted and monitored by hospitals. However, because of staffing shortages and stricter FDA regulations, there has been a major shift from in-house reprocessing to use of third-party reprocessing companies. These private companies now reprocess more than 100 types of SUDs, including those from our institution and other major hospitals.

What Not to Waste

Three categories of devices currently lend themselves to reprocessing. Class I devices have a relatively low associated risk to patients and include elastic bandages, pressure infuser bags, tourniquet cuffs, and general-use surgical scissors. These are exempt from premarket submission requirements. Approximately 65% to 75% of reprocessed SUDs fall into Class II (medium risk) which requires submission of a premarket notification report providing evidence of equivalence to devices already on the market in terms of safety, effectiveness, and intended use. Class II devices include pulse oximeter sensors, ultrasound catheters, drills, compression sleeves, and most laparoscopic equipment. The last group, Class III (high risk) devices, requires valid scientific data proving safety and effectiveness, in addition to a satisfactory inspection of the reprocessing facility in order to obtain FDA premarket approval. Devices that fall into this category are balloon angioplasty catheters, percutaneous tissue ablation electrodes, and implanted infusion pumps. Given the high patient risk associated with Class III devices and the strenuous approval process, most health care organizations refrain from reprocessing these items. FDA's postmarket activities involve inspection of reprocessing establishments and reviewing device safety reports, including reports of adverse events. (A complete listing of reprocessed devices is available on the FDA Web site at http://www.fda.gov/CDRH/reprocessing/510ksearch.html.)

Global and Local Savings

In 2002, approximately 25% of U.S. hospitals used at least one type of reprocessed SUD.[3] Larger hospitals have been more likely to reprocess equipment, with 45% of large hospitals (>250 beds) participating compared with only 13.3% of small hospitals (<50 beds).[3] This disparity, which has been increasing during the past five years, is likely due to a parallel trend toward heightened awareness at universities and teaching hospitals regarding the harmful effects of medical waste disposal in landfills. The resource constraints of these small hospitals may be an additional factor. However, we expect that the number of institutions engaging in reprocessing activities will continue to increase as awareness of the environmental impact of traditional waste disposal techniques spreads.

In addition to the environmental concerns, many hospitals have been struck hard by the current economic crises, with 2008–2009 profit margins at an all-time low. Given these financial concerns, hospitals are increasingly attracted to reprocessing because of its associated 50% reduction of medical device costs compared with purchasing new equipment. In 2008 alone, there was a 20% increase in hospital utilization of reprocessing services offered by one leading reprocessing service, and associated cost savings of $138,142,000 nationwide.[6] This represented 4,300,000 pounds (2,150 tons) of medical waste diverted from local landfills.[6] During the last 20 years of operation, this reprocessor has enabled $1 billion in savings in

Another Way to Reduce Medical Waste

[While] recycling is helpful, even reprocessed disposables eventually must be thrown away, said Dr. Rafael Andrade, a general thoracic surgeon at the University of Minnesota Medical Center, Fairview, who spoke at the recent Practice Greenhealth workshop [in May 2010]. The bigger goal, he said, should be to resume the old practice of relying on permanently reusable equipment. "We're just trying to undo a lot of the damage we've done," Dr. Andrade said.

Ingfei Chen,
"In a World of Throwaways, Making a Dent in Medical Waste,"
New York Times, *July 5, 2010.*

supply hosts and eliminated 24 million pounds of waste for its 1,700-member health care facilities.[6]

Cost savings differ from one institution to the next depending on types and quantity of devices reprocessed. Across the board, however, hospitals are observing significant savings which are being channeled into badly needed medical infrastructure or services. For instance, Banner Health in Phoenix also reported a total savings of $1,494,050 across 12 months from reprocessing operating room devices, compression sleeves, catheters, open but unused devices, and pulse oximeters.[1] This should be of particular interest to teaching hospitals, which provide over 40% of charity care in the United States and can divert the net savings from reprocessing to cover costs incurred from providing this unpaid service. Savings could also be used to fund needed research and employee-initiated projects.

Patient Safety

As mentioned earlier, one barrier to the widespread adoption of reprocessing is its potential impact on patient safety. Safety concerns include the possible malfunction of devices, the risk of infectious diseases, and the ethical dilemma reprocessing presents given the absence of patient consent to use of such devices as part of treatment. Many physicians and politicians have lobbied for legislation requiring written patient consent, documentation of all reprocessed SUDs used during treatment, and stricter systems of tracking SUD failures and injuries, while holding reprocessors fully liable for any adverse events.

The government has responded to these concerns by conducting several investigations and hearings about the reprocessing of SUDs and has introduced stricter regulations at all levels of production. Most notably, the Medical Device User Fee and Modernization Act (MDUMFA) of 2002 was enacted, requiring that all reprocessed SUDs be labeled and have the identification of the reprocessor. MDUMFA also created more stringent FDA oversight of reprocessed SUDs than had been present in the past. In January 2008, the U.S. Government Accountability Office (GAO) released a report entitled *Reprocessed Single-Use Medical Devices: FDA Oversight Has Increased, and Available Information Does Not Indicate That Use Presents an Elevated Health Risk.*[7] In this report, the GAO outlined steps taken by the FDA since 2000 to improve its supervision and regulation of reprocessing, including additional requirements for pre- and post-market approval and easier and more detailed adverse-effect-reporting mechanisms.[7] More important, GAO concluded that although available FDA data fail to allow for rigorous in-depth comparisons, reprocessed SUDs do not present an increased health risk when compared with new, non-reprocessed devices.[7] Of the 434 adverse events re-

ported to the FDA between 2003 and 2006 in which reprocessed SUDs were identified, only 65 actually did involve a reprocessed device, and all adverse events were similar to those
reported for new devices.[7]

Implications for AMCs

U.S. medical schools and teaching hospitals have become the
center for cutting-edge research, technology development, and
highly skilled health professional training. They have spear-
headed patient advocacy and safety issues leading to significant changes in health care delivery today. These efforts have
also been channeled into promoting green health care practices such as recycling, mercury elimination, and energy conservation in an attempt not only to protect our environment
but also to join public health efforts in preventive care.[2] Today, because of these initiatives, almost all AMCs have extensive recycling projects which have trickled down into the communities they serve. Reprocessing not only provides another
arena for promoting green practices but also offers AMCs a
chance to proactively reduce the volume of waste stream by
safely reusing sterilized, repackaged devices that previously
would have been discarded after a single use.

We have discussed both the environmental benefits and
cost savings associated with this practice and highlighted how
savings could be channeled into other avenues. In addition to
this, the relatively new status of reprocessing as a green health
care practice makes it an interesting and needed subject for
research. Faculty could create research projects for medical
students and resident staff that revolve around issues of ac-
ceptance, use, medical device errors, cost effectiveness, and
medical-legal issues that extend over a period of time. Such
research will be helpful in augmenting the existing limited literature and will help shape future health care practices espe-

cially in the fields of surgery, obstetrics-gynecology, emergency medicine, intensive care, and internal medicine, which all rely significantly on SUDs.

Centers interested in reprocessing should consider internal education of employees and students before initiation to maximize use and benefits. We have found that U.S. reprocessors have a strong environmental mission and operate transparently. They offer random factory site visits, conduct exhaustive testing of reprocessed devices, are registered with the FDA, and have adequate liability insurance coverage. It is important that similar high standards of service and production are upheld by any potential reprocessing organization that a hospital is interested in using. Though no regulatory oversight is perfect, our experience is that the reprocessing of SUDs currently has strong oversight to help ensure high-quality standards and patient safety.

Conclusion

Health care can contribute to creating a livable planet by reducing the substantial amount of medical waste it produces. Reprocessing is one strategy to accomplish this. The practice has a reliable safety record of excellence identical to that of new equipment, while being friendlier to the environment. Reprocessing offers health care institutions a solution to reduce waste and to reduce costs; as such, it should be explored.

Acknowledgments

The authors wish to thank Hugh Waters (Johns Hopkins Center for Green Healthcare) and Gary Cohen (Healthcare Without Harm) for their guidance and support of this research.

Funding/Support

Funding was provided by an unrestricted research gift from Mr. and Mrs. Chad and Nissa Richison.

Other disclosures

None.

Ethical approval

Not applicable.

References

1 Diconsiglio J. Reprocessing SUDs reduces waste, costs. Mater Manag Health Care. 2008;17:40–42.

2 Kwakye G, Brat G, Makary M. Green practices for surgical healthcare. Arch Surg. In press.

3 United States Department of Health and Human Services. Food and Drug Administration. Center for Devices and Radiological Health. Executive Summary: Survey on the Reuse and Reprocessing of Single-Use Devices (SUDs) in U.S. Hospitals. Available at: http://www.fda.gov/cdrh/ reprocessing/survey-execsum.html. Accessed January 14, 2009.

4 Selvey D. Medical device reprocessing: Is it good for your organization? Infect Control Today. January 1, 2001. Available at: http://www.infectioncontroltoday.com/articles/ 111feat1.html. Accessed January 12, 2009.

5 United States Department of Health and Human Services. Food and Drug Administration. Center for Devices and Radiological Health. Reprocessing of Single Used Devices: Definitions. Available at: http://www.fda.gov/Cdrh/ reprocessing/definitions.html. Accessed January 13, 2009.

6 Ascent Healthcare Solutions. Hospitals benefit from sustainability initiatives with more than $138 million in savings in 2008 [press release]. January 12, 2009. Available at: http://www.ascenths.com/docs/press/2008_year-end_011209.pdf. Accessed January 14, 2009.

7 United States Government Accountability Office. Report to the Committee on Oversight and Government Reform, House of Representatives. Reprocessed Single-Use Medical Devices: FDA Oversight Has Increased, and Available Information Does Not Indicate That Use Presents an Elevated Health Risk. Washington, DC: United States Government Accountability Office. January 31, 2008.

Periodical and Internet Sources Bibliography

The following articles have been selected to supplement the diverse views presented in this chapter.

Ingfei Chen	"In a World of Throwaways, Making a Dent in Medical Waste," *New York Times*, July 5, 2010.
Joe David	"Trash: America's Best Bet for Energy Independence," *Christian Science Monitor*, February 1, 2010.
Bonnie DeSimone	"Rewarding Recyclers, and Finding Gold in the Garbage," *New York Times*, February 21, 2006.
Peter Fairley	"Garbage In, Megawatts Out," *Technology Review*, July 2, 2008.
Grand Rapids Press	"Single-Stream Recycling Means No Excuse for Not Recycling," July 20, 2010.
Aaron Kase	"Trash Compactor Contract Filthy, Controller Says," *PhillyNow* (blog), July 12, 2010. http://blogs.philadelphiaweekly.com/phillynow.
Leslie Kaufman	"Nudging Recycling from Less Waste to None," *New York Times*, October 19, 2009.
Brendan I. Koerner	"Can We Turn Garbage into Energy?," Slate.com, January 2, 2008. www.slate.com.
Scott Learn	"Landfill Looks at Turning Portland Trash into Fuel," *Oregonian*, July 27, 2010.
Mary Mazzoni	"Is Burning Trash Bad?" Earth911.com, August 2, 2010. http://Earth911.com.
David Schaper	"Solar Compactors Make Mincemeat of Trash," NPR.org, July 17, 2007. www.npr.org.
Matt Viser	"Solar-Powered Compactors Press the Mess in Boston," *Boston Globe*, July 26, 2006.

For Further Discussion

Chapter 1

1. Is there a garbage crisis in the United States? Peter Lehner maintains that there is. In her viewpoint, Jane Chastain argues that there is not a crisis. Read both viewpoints to inform your opinion on the subject.

2. Graham Land contends that the Great Pacific Garbage Patch is an environmental catastrophe. Jay L. Wile argues that the dangers are exaggerated. After reading both viewpoints, which author do you agree with and why? What should be done about the garbage patch?

3. Many communities are considering a plastic bag tax or ban. Do you support such legislation? Read viewpoints by Marc Basnight and Lenore Skenazy to illuminate the pros and cons.

Chapter 2

1. The first four viewpoints of this chapter examine the benefits of and problems with recycling. After reading all four, do you think recycling is worth the resources it requires? Use information from the viewpoints to support your answer.

2. In his viewpoint, James Thayer asserts that mandatory recycling wastes time and money. Chris Bristol contends that it is the right thing to do. Should individuals be forced to recycle?

3. The efficacy of pay-as-you-throw programs is in question. Raphael Gang and Scot Matayoshi find them to be a viable solution to the waste problem. Richard Olson Jr. re-

jects such programs as inefficient. Would you welcome a pay-as-you-throw program in your community? Why or why not?

Chapter 3

1. The reprocessing of nuclear waste is a contentious subject. Read viewpoints from William Tucker and the Union of Concerned Scientists to learn about the topic. Do you agree with Tucker that reprocessing is the solution to the problem of nuclear waste disposal? Or do you think re-processing is not an effective option? Explain your answer.

2. Do you concur with President Obama's decision to close down the Yucca Mountain waste facility? Read viewpoints by Timothy Noah and Jack Spencer to illuminate both sides of the issue.

3. After reading the viewpoints about the benefits and pit-falls of recycling e-waste, outline the pros and cons of the practice. How can electronic recycling be improved? Is it widely available in your neighborhood?

Chapter 4

1. This chapter explores several strategies that aim to reduce waste and save money. After reading the viewpoints in this chapter, pick the one that seems most promising to you. Why do you think this practice or technology has poten-tial to reduce waste? What are the drawbacks to your choice?

2. Which of the strategies covered in this chapter is practiced in your community? How effective is it? If your commu-nity does not utilize any of the strategies or technologies discussed in this chapter, which do you feel would work in your area?

Organizations to Contact

The editors have compiled the following list of organizations concerned with the issues debated in this book. The descriptions are derived from materials provided by the organizations. All have publications or information available for interested readers. The list was compiled on the date of publication of the present volume; the information provided here may change. Be aware that many organizations take several weeks or longer to respond to inquiries, so allow as much time as possible.

American Coal Ash Association (ACAA)

15200 E. Girard Avenue, Suite 3050, Aurora, CO   80014
(720) 870-7897 • fax: (720) 870-7889
e-mail: info@acaa-usa.org
website: www.acaa-usa.org

The American Coal Ash Association (ACAA) is a trade organization that advocates for the sound management and environmentally responsible use of coal combustion products. To promote education on coal ash recycling and other industry issues, the ACAA co-hosts "The World of Coal Ash," an international symposium that occurs every two years. The organization also coordinates workshops, seminars, and lectures led by worldwide experts to disseminate information on recycling coal ash. The ACAA publishes a biannual magazine, *ASH at Work*, and an e-newsletter for members, *The Phoenix*, as well as policy briefs, informational fact sheets, handbooks, and studies. The ACAA website offers breaking news, press releases, and a calendar of upcoming events.

Earth Justice

426 Seventeenth Street, 6th Floor, Oakland, CA   94612
(800) 584-6460 • fax: (510) 550-6740
e-mail: info@earthjustice.org
website: earthjustice.org

Earth Justice is a nonprofit public-interest law firm that fights for environmental justice and the full implementation of environmental laws and regulations. The organization has provided legal representation to a number of conservation and environmental groups, including the Natural Resources Defense Council (NRDC), the Sierra Club, and the Wilderness Society. It also lobbies to strengthen federal environmental laws and create policies that will protect endangered species and pristine natural land. Earth Justice publishes a monthly e-newsletter, *e.brief*, which explores relevant environmental issues and provides updates on recent cases. The Earth Justice website offers access to the latest press releases and *Unearthed*, a blog that shares the latest news and facilitates discussion on environmental and legal topics.

Energy Recovery Council
1730 Rhode Island Avenue NW, Suite 700
Washington, DC 20036
(202) 467-6240
e-mail: info@energyrecoverycouncil.org
website: www.energyrecoverycouncil.org

The Energy Recovery Council is an American trade organization that represents the waste-to-energy industry and communities that own waste-to-energy facilities. One of the group's key objectives is to educate the public, local and state policy makers, and the media on the benefits of waste-to-energy technology. The Energy Recovery Council's website provides links to the latest news, directories of waste-to-energy facilities, industry fact sheets, commentary and op-eds, and reports on the latest research and data.

Environmental Defense Fund (EDF)
1875 Connecticut Avenue NW, Suite 600
Washington, DC 20009
(800) 684-3322 • fax: (212) 505-2375
website: www.edf.org

Established in 1967, the Environmental Defense Fund (EDF) is a nonprofit environmental advocacy group based in the United States that focuses on global warming, ecosystem restoration, clean oceans, and human health. Since it was founded by scientists, the EDF is committed to sound scientific research to address environmental problems. One of the areas EDF has made a valuable contribution to influencing public policy is the recognition of climate global change as an urgent problem. The EDF website features blogs, podcasts, and commentary on the latest environmental issues as well as archives of *Solutions*, its quarterly newsletter.

Environmental Protection Agency (EPA)

Ariel Rios Building, 1200 Pennsylvania Avenue NW
Washington, DC   20004
(202) 272-0167
website: www.epa.gov

The Environmental Protection Agency (EPA) is a US governmental agency that is tasked with protecting America's natural environment and safeguarding human health. The key responsibility of the EPA is to write and enforce environmental regulations. Established in 1970, the agency also conducts environmental research, provides assessments on environmental problems, and offers education on environmental policy and practices. The EPA works closely with local, state, and tribal governments to offer feedback and guidance on environmental policies and problems. On the EPA website, individuals can sign up for the monthly newsletter, *Go Green!*, and find a listing of environmental laws and regulations; updates on recent programs and initiatives; transcripts of speeches, seminars, and testimony; and in-depth research on environmental issues.

International Energy Agency (IEA)

9 rue de la Fédération, Paris   75015
    France
+33 1 40 57 65 00 • fax: +33 1 40 57 65 59
e-mail: info@iea.org
website: www.iea.org

The International Energy Agency (IEA) is an intergovernmental association that advises its twenty-eight member countries on issues of energy policy and clean energy. The IEA focuses on finding solutions for its members on energy security, economic development, and environmental protection, especially on climate change. The IEA conducts energy research and statistical compilation to assess the current state of the energy market and future trends in the industry; disseminates the latest energy news and policy analyses; and provides well-researched recommendations to member states. The organization publishes numerous in-depth reports offering insight on the energy industry and specific energy topics, as well as a monthly newsletter, *IEA Open Energy Technology Bulletin*, which provides regular updates on energy security and environmental issues.

Keep America Beautiful (KAB)
1010 Washington Boulevard, Stamford, CT 06901
(203) 659-3000 • fax: (203) 659-3001
e-mail: info@kab.org
website: www.kab.org

Keep America Beautiful (KAB) is a volunteer-based, community-action organization that aims to improve the environment. KAB has developed and implemented programs that bring communities together to generate improved environmental policies and stewardship in three main areas—litter prevention, recycling and waste reduction, and beautification and community greening. Another key activity of KAB is public education programs to raise awareness of recycling and waste reduction. KAB publishes an e-newsletter, *Community Matters*, and the organization's Curbside Value Partnership Program offers a quarterly newsletter, *Bin Buzz*, which can be accessed through the KAB website.

Natural Resources Defense Council (NRDC)
40 West Twentieth Street, New York, NY 10011
(212) 727-2700 • fax: (212) 727-1773
e-mail: nrdcinfo@nrdc.org
website: www.nrdc.org

Established in 1970, the Natural Resources Defense Council (NRDC) is an environmental action organization that mobilizes lawyers, activists, policy makers, and scientists to protect wildlife and the natural environment. The NRDC's aims include reducing waste, improving and facilitating the spread of recycling programs, eliminating the dumping of toxic chemicals and solid waste on land and in the water, and reducing pollution of all kinds. NRDC.tv, which can be accessed on the organization's website, offers video and audio on a range of environmental subjects. The website also hosts *The Switchboard*, a blog from NRDC's environmental experts, and *OnEarth*, a blog that covers the latest news from *OnEarth* magazine, a publication that explores major environmental issues and NRDC initiatives.

Nuclear Energy Institute (NEI)

1776 I Street NW, Suite 400, Washington, DC   20006
(202) 739-8000 • fax: (202) 785-4019
website: www.nei.org

The Nuclear Energy Institute (NEI) is a policy organization that works to implement pro-nuclear policies and advocates for the use of nuclear energy and technologies. The NEI is active in developing regulations that benefit both the nuclear industry and communities and lobbying for pro-industry legislation. The organization also raises awareness of the benefits of nuclear power to the public, providing public relations and educational services to promote the industry. The NEI website offers access to a library of documents, including statistics, fact sheets, research papers, policy briefs, and in-depth reports on nuclear power and the nuclear power industry. It also provides a link to the NEI's bimonthly newsletter, *Nuclear Energy Insight*, which examines emerging technologies and policy opinions and updates.

Plastic Pollution Coalition

2150 Allston Way, Suite 460, Berkeley, CA   94704
(510) 394-5772
e-mail: contact@plasticpollutioncoalition.org
website: http://plasticpollutioncoalition.org

The Plastic Pollution Coalition is a network of organizations, businesses, and activists working together to reduce and eventually eliminate pollution caused by disposable plastic. One of its main objectives is to raise awareness of the environmental dangers of plastic pollution and facilitate a shift to more environmentally responsible practices. Banning plastic bags is a key initiative sponsored by the network. The Plastic Pollution Coalition website links to video of recent lectures, presentations, and speeches on plastic pollution.

Practice Greenhealth

12335 Sunrise Valley Drive, Suite 680, Reston, VA   20191
(888) 688-3332 • fax: (866) 379-8705
e-mail: info@practicegreenhealth.org
website: www.practicegreenhealth.org

Practice Greenhealth is a membership and networking organization for the health care community. Its primary focus is on developing and encouraging sustainable, environmentally friendly practices for the industry, including the reprocessing of medical equipment. Practice Greenhealth hosts seminars and lectures to disseminate information about the latest eco-friendly strategies in the health care field as well as forums to share ideas and collaborate on green initiatives. One such program is Greening the OR, which focuses on products and practices in operating rooms that can reduce the amount of medical waste generated. Practice Greenhealth publishes a weekly e-newsletter, *Greenhealth eNews*, which offers the latest news in the field and updates on current initiatives.

Save the Plastic Bag Coalition

350 Bay Street, Suite 100-328, San Francisco, CA   94133
website: www.savetheplasticbag.com

The Save the Plastic Bag Coalition was founded in 2008 to advocate for the use of plastic bags, paper bags, and reusable bags. It presents research on the effects of plastic- and paper-bag pollution to counter what it sees as propaganda against plastic bags. These studies can be found on the organization's website. Save the Plastic Bag Coalition acts legislatively in its home state of California to ensure that municipalities considering a plastic bag tax or ban exercise due diligence and policy makers know about their options. The group's website provides counterpoints to environmental groups seeking to eliminate the use of plastic and paper bags, working to correct misinformation and mythology.

Sierra Club
85 Second Street, 2nd Floor, San Francisco, CA 94105
(415) 977-5500 • fax: (415) 977-5799
e-mail: information@sierraclub.org
website: www.sierraclub.org

The Sierra Club is the oldest environmental organization in the United States. Its mission is to protect communities from environmental dangers, including waste pollution. To that end, the Sierra Club has formulated a Climate Recovery Agenda, defined as "a set of initiatives that will help cut carbon emissions 80 percent by 2050, reduce US dependence on foreign oil, create a clean-energy economy, and protect the nation's natural heritage, communities, and country from the consequences of global warming." The Sierra Club publishes a range of e-newsletters, including the *Insider*, which is considered the organization's flagship publication. The Sierra Club website links to blogs, video, Sierra Club radio, and publications, such as *Sierra Magazine*.

Solid Waste Association of North America (SWANA)
1100 Wayne Avenue, Suite 700, Silver Springs, MD 20910
(800) GO-SWANA • fax: (301) 589-7068
website: http://swana.org

The Solid Waste Association of North America (SWANA) is the trade organization for the solid waste industry. Its mission is to keep industry professionals updated on the latest technology, practices, and initiatives through seminars, training, conferences, and other professional forums. SWANA's Applied Research Foundation conducts research on solid waste issues of interest to its members, including environmental impacts and practices. For members, an extensive e-library of studies, research, and papers is available on the group's website.

Bibliography of Books

Maggie Black and Ben Fawcett — *The Last Taboo: Opening the Door on the Global Sanitation Crisis.* London: EarthScan, 2008.

John D'Agata — *About a Mountain.* New York: W.W. Norton, 2010.

Curtis Ebbesmeyer and Eric Scigliano — *Flotsametrics and the Floating World: How One Man's Obsession with Runaway Sneakers and Rubber Ducks Revolutionized Ocean Science.* New York: Smithsonian Books, 2009.

Ylenia E. Farrugia, ed. — *Nuclear Waste: Disposal and Liability Issues.* Hauppauge, NY: Nova Science Publishers, 2011.

Christian S. Gallo and Lorenzo F. Rossi, eds. — *Recycling: New Research.* Hauppauge, NY: Nova Science Publishers, 2009.

Christine E. Gudorf and James E. Huchingson — *Boundaries: A Casebook in Environmental Ethics.* 2nd ed. Washington, DC: Georgetown University Press, 2010.

A.K. Haghi, ed. — *Waste Management: Research Advances to Convert Waste to Wealth.* Hauppauge, NY: Nova Science Publishers, 2010.

Bonnie Henderson — *Strand: An Odyssey of Pacific Ocean Debris.* Corvallis: Oregon State University Press, 2008.

Donovan Hohn   *Moby-Duck: An Accidental Odyssey.* New York: Viking, 2010.

Trevor Letcher and Daniel Vallero, eds.   *Waste: A Handbook for Management.* Burlington, MA: Academic Press, 2011.

Christian V. Loeffe, ed.   *Trends in Conservation and Recycling of Resources.* Hauppauge, NY: Nova Science Publishers, 2007.

Daniel D. Lowell, ed.   *Coal Combustion Waste: Management and Beneficial Uses.* Hauppauge, NY: Nova Science Publishers, 2010.

Martin V. Melosi   *The Sanitary City: Environmental Services in Urban America from Colonial Times to the Present.* Pittsburgh, PA: University of Pittsburgh Press, 2008.

Cecilia Minden   *Reduce, Reuse, and Recycle.* Ann Arbor, MI: Cherry Lake Publishers, 2010.

Skye Moody   *Washed Up: The Curious Journeys of Flotsam and Jetsam.* New York: MJF Books, 2009.

Charlene J. Nielsen, ed.   *Recycling: Processes, Costs, and Benefits.* Hauppauge, NY: Nova Science Publishers, 2011.

Laura Pritchett, ed.   *Going Green: True Tales from Gleaners, Scavengers, and Dumpster Divers.* Norman: University of Oklahoma Press, 2009.

Rebecca R. Scott   *Removing Mountains: Extracting Nature and Identity in the Appalachian Coalfields.* Minneapolis: University of Minnesota Press, 2010.

Daniel J. Sherman   *Not Here, Not There, Not Anywhere: Politics, Social Movements, and the Disposal of Low-Level Radioactive Waste.* Washington, DC: RFF Press, 2011.

Lucy Siegle   *Recycle: The Essential Guide.* 2nd ed. London: Black Dog Publishing, 2010.

Richard B. Stewart and Jane B. Stewart   *Fuel Cycle to Nowhere: U.S. Law and Policy on Nuclear Waste.* Nashville, TN: Vanderbilt University Press, 2011.

Tristram Stuart   *Waste: Uncovering the Global Food Scandal.* New York: W.W. Norton, 2009.

Peter H. Telone, ed.   *Fly Ash Reuse, Environmental Problems, and Related Issues.* Hauppauge, NY: Nova Science Publishers, 2010.

J. Samuel Walker   *The Road to Yucca Mountain: The Development of Radioactive Waste Policy in the United States.* Berkeley: University of California Press, 2009.

Index

A

ABC News, 164–169
Ackerman, Frank, 95
Adams, Jack, 191–194
AERC Recycling Solutions, 163
Africa
  discarded e-waste, 159
  food shortage crisis, 22
  plastic bag pollution, 57
  plastic bag taxes, 20
  trash production comparison, 67–68
Alexandria (VA) use of RFID recycling bins, 102
Algalita Marine Research Foundation, 41–43
Alliance Federated Energy, 201
Aluminum cans, 21, 23
  deposit laws, 28
  magnetic field separation, 81–82
  recycling, 64, 78
American Chemistry Council (ACC), 175, 178
Apple, Inc., 85
AREVA (French nuclear waste conglomerate), 126–128, 130–131
Arsenic
  e-waste disposal issue, 119
  mining firm use of, 192
  wood treated-arsenic, 161
Arsenic-contaminated water
  coal ash arsenic content, 157
  Edisto River issues, 155–156
  landfill concentrations, 150–152

mine wastewater, 193
mining firm use of, 192
wood treatment with arsenic, 161
Ashby, Jeff, 87
Asian Trash Trail, 41
Association for Automatic Identification and Mobility, 103
Atomic Licensing and Safety Board (NRC), 139
Australia, anti-plastic bag action, 20
Austria
  plastics recycling, 84
  recycling trends, 76

B

Balko, Radley, 91
Bangladesh
  food shortage crisis, 22
  plastic bags outlawed, 20
Barges, rubbish-laden, 79
Bartelme, Tony, 149–157
Basel Action Network, 159, 166
Basnight, Marc, 50–54
Benjamin, Daniel K., 25, 26–27, 91, 93–94
Besso, Bob, 82
BetterEarth.org project, 91
Beverage bottles. See Plastic beverage bottles
Biddle, Michael, 83–84
BigBelly Solar (MA), 188
Bloggers/blogging, 45, 46, 56, 101, 105
Bloomberg, Michael, 91

Blue Ribbon Commission on America's Nuclear Future, 142
Bonlender, Ron, 99
Bottles. *See* Plastic beverage bottles
Bradley, Anthony B., 70–74
Braungart, Michael, 73
Bristol, Chris, 96–100
British Petroleum (BP), oil spill, 175, 178
Brown paper supermarket bags, 22
"Building Consensus and Planning for Unit Pricing" (EPA), 114
Building Owners and Managers Association (WA), 93
Bush, George W., 15, 133, 137, 139

C

California
   e-waste problems, 119–120
   Garbage Mass, 43
   Grocers Association, 19
   Long Beach coastal studies, 42
   Los Angeles recycling, 91
   Norcal Waste Systems, 80
   PAYT programs, 61
   plastic bag ban, 19–20
   sanitary landfills, 39
   Silicon Valley Toxics Coalition, 85
Canada
   arsenic-tainted mine wastewater, 193
   electrobiochemical gasification, 200
   household waste recycling, 68
   importation of tracer material, 124
   plastics shipped to, 183

Cancer
   arsenic dangers, 154
   coal ash landfill dangers, 151, 153
   e-waste risks, 159
   EPA death estimates, 94
   landfill chemical leaks, 29–32
Cans. *See* Aluminum cans
Carbon dioxide (CO2) pollution, 23, 53, 77, 136
Cardboard recyclables, 81, 93
Carter, Jimmy, 123, 124–125, 136
Caruso, Troy, 199
Cato Institute, 92
Certified-recycler certificate (EPA), 167–168
Charlottesville (VA), illegal dumping, 114–115
Chastain, Jane, 25–28
Chen, Ingfei, 213
Chesley, Chip, 115–116
China
   anti-plastic bag action, 20
   carbon emission reduction motivation, 53
   discarded e-waste, 159, 166
   EBR technology, 192
   food shortage crisis, 22
   migrant workers cottage industry, 85
   plastics recycling, 83–84
   plastics shpped to, 183
   shipping recyclables to, 84–85
Chu, Steven, 122
Clean Air Council, 31
Clemson University, 91, 93–94
Cleveland (OH)
   economic considerations, 105
   recycling revenue generation, 103

use of RFID recycling bins, 101–102

Coeur d'Alene (WA) recycling, 179–180

Coifman, Jon, 57

Cole, Chris, 63–66

Collins, Dan, 56

"The Comeback Country" (Gross), 188

Competitive Enterprise Institute, 91

Computer Recycling of Virginia, 163

Concord Monitor article, 115–116

Concord (NH) PAYT programs, 115–116

Congress (US)
e-waste handling action, 162
Nuclear Waste Policy Act, 15

Consumption encouraged by recycling, 67–69

Cordeiro, Leo, 205

Cradle to Cradle: Remaking the Way We Make Things (McDonough and Braungart), 73, 86–87

Curbside recycling (US), 28, 78–80, 89

D

D'Agostino Supermarkets, 56

Dawe, Andy, 85–86

"De-Mystifying the Great Pacific Garbage Patch" (NOAA Marine Debris Program), 47

Dell, Inc., 85

DEQ (Department of Environmental Quality), 160, 163

DHEC (Department of Health and Environmental Control), 151, 155–157

Dickson County (TN) lawsuits, 29–32

Diedrich, Roger, 161, 163

Dinkins, David, 91

Division of Waste Collection (OH), 105

Downcycling of recyclables, 70, 83

Duales System Deutschland (DSD), 79

E

E-waste (electronic waste)
environmental recycling benefits, 158–163
EPA discarded waste data, 158–159
Exporting Harm video, 166
hazardousness of, 165–166
problems caused by, 119
recycling, 23, 37–38
shipping to Third World countries, 159, 162
Third World country recycling dangers, 164–169
US recycling program criticism, 120
Virginia's allowance of dumping, 160

EarthJustice group, 153–154

Eastern Garbage Patch, 41

Ebbesmeyer, Curtis, 45, 47–49

EBR technology. See electrobiochemical (EBR) technology

The Economist magazine, 75–88

Edisto River (SC) ash contamination, 155–156

Edler, Dave, 97, 98–99

"Eight Great Myths of Recycling" (Benjamin), 26–27
Electrobiochemical (EBR) technology, 190–194
  benefits of, 191–192
  described, 191
  mechanics of, 192–193
  potential benefits of, 193–194
Electronic Waste Recycling Act (2003), 119–120
Elopak waste-sorting systems, 82
Energy, Department of (US), 15, 127–130, 133, 135
EnviroArc, gasification start-up, 200
Environment News Service (ENS), 29–32
Environmental Cleanup Coalition, 44
Environmental consequences of plastic bags, 51–52
Environmental Integrity Project, 156
Environmental Protection Agency (EPA)
  ash waste tainted groundwater survey, 150
  cancer-related death estimates, 94
  certified-recycler certificate, 167–168
  coal ash landfill study, 151, 153–154
  coal combustion product classification, 143
  discarded e-waste data, 158–159
  drinking water toxicity limits, 32
  intolerance for "paid trash hack," 113, 114

materials management goals, 88
paper recycling toxic substances, 26, 28
PAYT essay, 110
radioactive level regulations, 134
recycling trends report, 65
sanitary landfill standards, 38
US carbon emissions estimates, 77
waste generation report, 37
waste-to-energy process emissions, 31
Environmental Quality, Department of (DEQ), 160
"EPA Data Reveal Far Reach of Toxic Coal Ash Threats" (Earth Justice), 153
Estée Lauder, packaging toxicity concerns, 87
Ethanol fuel, 71–73
Europe
  e-cycling efforts, 120
  packaging directive, 87–88
  PAYT programs, 109
  recycling trends, 76
  take-back laws, 83
Exporting Harm video, 166

F

"Facts About the Plastic Bag Pandemic" (Reusit.com), 52
Fighting Creek landfill (Idaho), 181–182
Fisheries, protection of, 53
Fly ash landfills and ponds
  arsenic-contaminated water, 150–152

coal ash waste disposal, 143–148
health hazards created by, 149–157
Indiana/Montana coal ash dumping, 157
"killer smog" contributions, 152
SCE&G issues, 150–152, 154–156
Food-grade bottle-to-bottle recycling, 83
Ford, Gerald, 123, 124–125
Franklin Associates, 89, 92
Freedom of Information Act (South Carolina), 150
Fresh Kills swamp (Staten Island), 94
Fuji-Keizai USA, 206

G

G. Dockham Trucking Co., 116
Gallo, Dan, 159–160, 162
Gang, Raphael, 107–111
Garbage crisis (US)
evidence for, 21–24
lack of evidence for, 25–28
Geoplasma, gasification start-up, 200, 205
George Mason University, 91
Giuliani, Rudy, 91
Glavin, Bob, 166
Global Alliance for Incinerator Alternatives, 205
Global warming
carbon cap-and-trade system and, 148
fears of, 147
nuclear power revival and, 136

Good Morning America tv show, 46
Gore, Al, 93
Government Accountability Office (GAO), 162, 173
Great Britain
bottle recycling, 86
political landfill concerns, 84
recycling trends, 76
RFID recycling model, 102, 103–104
waste education officers, 104
WRAP recycling calculations, 77
"The Great Pacific Cleanup" (Stone), 42
Great Pacific Garbage Patch
alternative names for, 41, 44
camera surveillance, 175
cleanup speculation, 177
described, 46–47
Ebbesmeyer's size determination, 45, 47–49
ecological dangers of, 40, 42–43
exaggerations about problem, 45–49
formation of, 41
investigation of, 47–49
plastic bag component, 52
plastic vs. plankton composition, 52
viable solutions to, 44
Greece, anti-plastic bag action, 20
"Green dot" trademark, 79
Green Launches website (United Kingdom), 104, 105
Green Revolution, 22, 24
Green use of landfills, 38
Greenboozling, 70, 73–74
GreenFudge.org, 40

GreenMuze.com, 67–69
Greenpeace, 42
Greentoys.com, 71
Greenwashing trend
   description/consequences,
   71–72
   example of, 72–73
Gristede's food markets, 56
Gross, Daniel, 185–189

H

Hale, Matt, 88
Harris, Eric, 163
Hawaii
   Honolulu recycling programs,
   90
   PAYT programs, 107, 108–109
HDPE (type 2) plastic bottles, 81,
83
Health and Environmental Con-
trol, Department of (DHEC),
151, 155–157
Heartland Institute, 91
Heritage Foundation, 137
Hewlett-Packard, 85
Hill, Brock, 143–148
Hiroshima (Japan) atomic bomb,
123–124
HIV (human immunodeficiency
virus), 173
Holt, Beatrice, 30–32
Holt, Mary, 30–32
Honolulu (HI), recycling pro-
grams, 90
Hopkinton (NH) PAYT program,
116
Hospital Corporation of America,
173

Houghton, Robert, 162–163
Hutchinson, Alex, 72

I

Illegal dumping
   Charlottesville, Virginia, 114–
   115
   cost-benefit analyses inclusion,
   112
   EPA concerns about, 114
   PAYT and, 62
"In a World of Throwaways, Mak-
ing a Dent in Medical Waste"
(Chen), 213
Incineration of waste, 36, 72
India
   anti-plastic bag action, 20
   e-waste problems, 120
   EBR technology, 192
   food shortage crisis, 22
   nuclear reprocessing facilities,
   123
   polluting paper mills, 84
Indian Ocean, ocean-wide gyre, 42
Indiana coal ash dumping, 157
Institute for Humane Studies
   (George Mason University), 91
Institute of Scrap Recycling Industries (ISRI), 78, 163
International Dynetics, 201–202
International Institute for Environment and Development, 95
Iran, radioactive material processing, 125
Ireland
   cloth bag replacement, 108
   plastic bag usage reduction,
   107–108
   tax on plastic bags, 20, 57,
   108

"Is Recycling Worth It? PM Investigates Its Economic and Environmental Impact" (Hutchinson), 72
"Is the Solution to the U.S. Nuclear Waste Problem in France?" (Ling), 123
Israel, anti-plastic bag action, 20
Italy, anti-plastic bag action, 20

J

Jacobson, Mark Z., 72, 139
Jaczko, Gregory, 138
Japan
    Chinese waste import studies, 85
    Hiroshima atomic bomb, 123–124
    nuclear reprocessing facilities, 123
    take-back laws, 83
Jefferson, Thomas, 51, 53
Jobs, Steve, 85
Jordan, Chris, 22

K

Kamps, Kevin, 136
Kauffman, Rod, 93
Keep Evansville Beautiful campaign, 63
Kwakye, Gifty, 208–218

L

La Hague nuclear fuel reprocessing facility, 123
Land, Graham, 40–44
Landfills
    acidic liquids creation, 161

benefits of, 34–35
costs of operation, 109–110
dangers of, 29–32
Dickson County lawsuit, 29–32
energy usage, 72
EPA 2008 survey, 31
plastic bag pollution, 20
purposes of, 34
recycling rates, 65
relative safety of, 33–39
Terrace Heights (WA), 96, 98
toxin leaks, 29, 31–32
Waimanalo Gulch (HI), 109
waste manageability, 93–94
See also Fly ash landfills; Sanitary landfills
Lehner, Peter, 21–24
Leita, Mike, 97, 99
Ling, Katherine, 123
Longo, Joseph, 196–204, 207

M

Makary, Martin A., 208–218
Malthus, Thomas, 21–22, 24
Mandatory recycling
    civil liberties undermined by, 101–106
    debates about in North America, 105–106
    logistics of, 99
    political dynamics of, 98–99
    reduction of wastefulness, 96–100
    wastefulness of resources, 89–95
    Yakima (WA) concerns, 97–98
Marazzo, Paul, 199, 206
Marx, Christal, 63–66
Matayoshi, Scot, 107–111

Materialism encouraged by recycling, 67–69
Mayo Clinic, 52
McCain, John, 135
McDonough, William, 73, 86
McElroy, Wendy, 101–106
MeadWestvaco coal-burning industry, 154
Medical equipment reprocessing, 208–218
    implications for medical schools, 215–216
    local/global savings, 212–213
    patient safety concerns, 214–215
    reprocessing (defined), 210–211
    waste determination, 211–212
Medical waste disposal issues, 17, 172–173, 209, 212–213, 216
Michelsen Packaging (WA), 97
Michigan, PAYT programs, 61
Moon, Steve, 183–184
Moore, Charles J., 41, 43, 48
    See also Great Pacific Garbage Patch
Morris, Jeffrey, 77
"Motivated by a Tax, Irish Spurn Plastic Bags" (Rosenthal), 57
MSW (municipal solid waste), 65, 81
"Municipal Solid Wste Generation" (EPA), 37

N

National Academy of Sciences, 14–15, 134
National Center for Electronics Recycling, 161
National Ethanol Vehicle Coalition (NEVC), 72–73
National Hydrogen Association, 206
National Institute for Environmental Studies (Japan), 85
National Recycling Coalition (US), 73–74, 80
National Science Foundation (NSF), 200
Natural History journal, 46–47
Natural Resources Defense Council (NRDC), 21, 29, 57, 91
Netherlands, recycling trends, 76
Nevada Policy Research Institute, 90, 94
"New Fight Breaks Out on Nuclear Dump Site" (Tracy), 135
New York City
    Fresh Kills (Staten Island), 94
    PAYT programs, 61
    plastic bag issue, 56–57
    recycling program, 91
New York Sun newspaper, 55
New York Times article, 57
Nigeria, e-waste problems, 120
Nineteen Eighty-Four (Orwell), 105
NOAA Marine Debris Program, 47
Noah, Timothy, 132–136
Norcal Waste Systems, 80
North Atlantic, ocean-wide gyre, 42
North Carolina. See Outer Banks (NC) marine ecosystem
North Korea, radioactive material processing, 125
North Pacific, Subtropical Gyre, 41, 48

Novak, John T., 161

NRC. See Nuclear Regulatory Commission

Nuclear fuel waste reprocessing
AREVA's misleading claims, 127–129
global state of, 123
hoax of nuclear waste, 124–125
La Hague (France) facility, 123
negative viewpoint, 126–131
plutonium, 121, 124–125, 127–128, 130, 136
positive viewpoint, 121–125
reactor applications, 133–134
types of nuclear waste, 128
uranium-235, 122–124
uranium-238, 121–122, 124
usable material, 124
See also Yucca Mountain (NV) nuclear waste site proposal

Nuclear Regulatory Commission (NRC), 16
approved low-level waste sites, 129
Atomic Licensing and Safety Board, 139
halt to Yucca-related activities, 138–140
McCain's possible actions with, 135
new reactor applications, 136
review of DOE's Yucca permit, 141–142

Nuclear Waste Policy Act (1982), 15, 139

Nuzzi, Michael, 199–200

O

Obama, Barack
opinion of nuclear power, 132, 136
Yucca Mountain site debate, 16, 122, 127, 134–135

Ocean pollution. See Great Pacific Garbage Patch

Ocean-wide gyres, 42

Office of Technology Assessment (US), 27

Olson, Richard, Jr., 112–116

Oregon State University, 47

Orwell, George, 105

Outer Banks (NC) marine ecosystem, 50–51, 53–54

Owens, Ronnie, 105

P

Pacific Northwest. See Seattle (WA); Spokane (WA) Recycling; Washington (state); Yakima County (WA) recycling

Pacific Ocean. See Great Pacific Garbage Patch; Outer Banks (NC) marine ecosystem

Packaging toxicity, 87

Parfitt, Julian, 76

"Pay-As-You-Throw" essay (EPA), 110

Pay-as-you-throw (PAYT) programs
affiliated trash costs, 109–110
benefits of, 110–111
categories of, 61
Concord (NH) situation, 115–116
criticism of, 62

disproportionate family penalization, 115
 environmental appeal of, 61–62
 in Hawaii, 107–109
 Hopkinton (NH) situation, 116
 lack of success of, 112–116
 strategic decisions, 114–115
 success of, 107–111
 waste strategies of, 110
PET (type 1) plastic bottles, 81, 83
Philadelphia (PA) recycling programs, 90
Pitts, Jim, 116
Plasco Energy, gasification start-up, 200
Plasma gasification trash conversion process, 195–207
 description, 197–198
 global interest in, 200–201
 investor interest, 198–200
 Joseph Longo's involvement, 196–204, 207
 technological viability of, 204–205
 See also Startech Environmental Corporation
Plastic bags
 anti-legislation stance, 56
 banning of, case against, 55–58
 banning of, case for, 50–54
 comprehensive law passage, 53–54
 downsides to, 57, 80
 environmental consequences, 51–52
 Ireland tax/Bangladesh ban, 20
 problem facts, 52

recycling vs. banning, 57–58
 San Francisco ban, 19–20
Plastic beverage bottles, 21–22
 PET/HDPE (type 2), 81, 83
 Seattle recycling, 93
 separation/recycling, 26
Plastic Debris, Rivers to Sea (Algalita Marine Research Foundation), 41–42
Plutonium, 121, 124–125, 127–128, 130, 136
Poss, Jim, 188
Progressive Investor magazine, 70, 73
Pronovost, Peter, 208–218
Property and Environment Research Center (PERC), Clemson University, 26, 28
Puckett, Jim, 159, 166–177
PyroGenesis, gasification start-up, 200

R

Rabanco/Allied Waste Industries (WA), 90
Radio-frequency identification (RFID)
 Cleveland recycling bins, 101–102
 described, 103
 Great Britain model, 102, 103–104
 United States objections, 106
Reagan, Ronald, 123
Reclamation of sanitary landfills, 38–39
Recovered Energy, gasification start-up, 200

Recycling
 aluminum cans, 21, 23, 28, 64, 78, 81–82
 cost inefficiencies, 103
 environmental benefits, 75–88
 environmental problems not solved by, 70–74
 free market dictates, 25
 historical background, 78
 as landfill alternative, 37–38
 materialism, consumption from, 67–69
 paper recycling process, 26
 PAYT programs, 61–62
 problems with, 27–28
 profile of recyclers, 68
 single-stream recycling, 180–184
 social responsibility aspect, 66
 three Rs equation, 69
 US preoccupation with, 26–27
 See also Mandatory recycling
"Reduce, Reuse, Recycle" saying, 174–176
Reid, Harry, 14, 122, 135, 138–142
"Reprocessing and Nuclear Waste" (Union of Concerned Scientists), 128
Reuseit.com, 52
Rhode Island, recycling costs, 91
Roberge, Steve, 182–183
Robertson, Scott, 99
Rocky Mountain Recycling, 87
Rohas, Elias, 90, 95
Rokkasho (Japan) nuclear reprocessing facility, 123
Roman, Lauren, 167–169
Rosenthal, Elisabeth, 57
Russo, Daniella, 174–178

S

San Francisco (CA)
 ban on plastic bags, 19–20
 curbside recycling, 80
Sandbrook, Richard, 95
Sanitary landfills
 alternatives to, 36–38
 EPA standards, 38
 locating, 35–36
 reclamation of, 38–39
Santee Cooper's Grainger coal plant, 151–152
Sargasso Sea, 42
SCE&G (South Carolina Electric and Gas)
 ash disposal operations, 151
 Candays coal plant, 154–155
 Congaree National Park landfill, 152
 Edisto River contamination, 155–156
 Wateree River plant, 150
Seattle (WA)
 Basel Action Network, 159
 citizen time spent recycling, 93
 curbside recycling expense, 89
 janitorial bills, 93
 recycling laws, 90–91
 religious nature of recycling, 95
Seattle Public Utilities survey, 92–93, 95
Seattle Stomp, 113–114
Seattle Times article, 95
Shipping recyclables to China, 84–85
Sicmar International, 206
Sierra Club, 161
Silicon Valley Toxics Coalition, 85

Single-stream recycling, 180–184
Single-use plastic, 174–178
SINTEF Norwegian research center, 82
Skenazy, Lenore, 55–58
Skumatz Economic Research Associates, 113
Social responsibility aspect of recycling, 66
Solar--powered trash compactors, 185–189
Solid Waste Management Department (WA), 181
Sound Resource Management (Washington state), 77
South Africa, anti-plastic bag action, 20
South Atlantic ocean-wide gyre, 42
South Pacific ocean-wide gyre, 42
Spencer, Jack, 137–142
Spokane (WA) Recycling, 183–184
Springston, Rex, 158–163
Stanford University, 72
Stant, Jeff, 156
Starbucks, packaging toxicity concerns, 87
Startech Environmental Corporation, 195–200, 203–204, 206
Stone, Daniel, 42
Sustainable Packaging Coalition, 87
Sziky, Victor, 206

T

Taiwan, anti-plastic bag action, 20
Target, packaging toxicity concerns, 87
Taylor, Jerry, 92

Taylor, Kevin, 179–184
Technology
  innovations in recycling, 87–88
  magnetic field conveyer belts, 81–82
  plasma gasification, 195–207
  role in recycling, 82–83
Technology Commercialization Office (University of Utah), 193–194
Terrace Heights landfill (WA), 96, 98
Thayer, James, 89–95
Thomas A. Roe Institute for Economic Policy Studies, 137
Three Mile Island nuclear plant accident, 136
Three Rs equation of recycling, 69
TiTech waste separation system, 82–83
Tracy, Tennille, 135
Trash Vortex, 41, 44
Trichlorethylene (TCE), 29–32, 30–32
"The Truth About Recycling" *(The Economist)*, 81
Tucker, William, 121–125

U

Union Leader article, 116
Union of Concerned Scientists, 126–131
United Kingdom
  household waste recycling, 68
  nuclear reprocessing facilities, 123
  trash sorting mandate, 104

United States
aluminum cans data, 21, 23
BP oil spill and cleanup, 175,
178
cancer deaths, 94
carbon emission reduction
motivation, 53
carbon emissions estimates, 77
consumer electronics spending, 164–165
curbside collection schemes,
78–79, 78–80
electronic device addiction,
119–120
foreign oil dependence, 19
fuel price crisis, 22
garbage crisis, evidence for,
21–24
garbage crisis, lack of evidence, 25–28
landfill capacity, 93–94
National Recycling Coalition,
73–74, 80
Nuclear Regulatory Commission, 129
PAYT programs, 61–62
plastic beverage bottles usage,
21–22
radioactive waste storage decision, 14–15
recycling preoccupation,
26–27
RFID chip monitoring objections, 106
tripling of municipal waste
collection, 76
See also Environmental Protection Agency
Uranium-235, 122–124
Uranium-238, 121–122, 124
U.S. Office of Technology Assessment, 27

Useful-Community-Develop
ment.org, 33–39

V

Van Beukering, Pieter, 84
Virginia
e-waste dumping allowance,
160
e-waste variety (data), 163
Sierra Club activities, 161

W

Waimanalo Gulch (HI) landfill,
109
Wal-Mart, packaging toxicity con-
cerns, 87
Wall Street Journal articles, 91,
135
Washington (state)
Michelsen Packaging, 97
PAYT programs, 61
Sound Resource Management,
77
See also Seattle (WA); Yakima
County (WA) recycling
Waste & Resources Action Pro-
gramme (WRAP) study, 76–77,
87
"Waste and Recycling Facts"
(Clean Air Council), 31
Waste education officers (Oxford,
England), 104
Waste Management Co. (Idaho),
181–182
Water Authority of Dickson
County (TN), 31–32
Wealth generated by garbage, 25

"What is RFID?" (Association for Automatic Identification and Mobility), 103

White, Angelicque, 47–49

"Why Plasma Gasification? Environmental FAQ" (Alliance Federated Energy), 201

Wile, Jay L., 45–49

Wilson, Monica, 205

Wisconsin Department of Health Services, 168

WNYC public radio, 58

Worldwatch Institute, 20

Wulf, Steve, 182–183

Y

Yakima County (WA) recycling
2003 landfill study, 96
2011 campaign issue, 99–100
Leita's opinion, 97
political dynamics of recycling, 98–99
recycling logistics, 99
role of leadership, 97–98

Yakima Waste Systems, 97–99

YouTube video, 46

Yucca Mountain Development Act (2002), 139

Yucca Mountain (NV) nuclear waste site proposal
2008 presidential debate, 16
alternatives to, 135–136
associated legislative actions, 140–142
attempts at shutting down, 123, 134–135
cancellation of, 127
Chu's comments about, 122
closing of, agreement, 132–136
closing of, disagreement, 137–142
negative health consequences, 14
Nevadan's opposition to, 15, 134, 142
new beginnings for, 140–142
NRC review of, 16

Z

Zooplankton, 41, 43